About This Book

Our purpose in this short book is to give readers a brief introduction to the basics of developmentally appropriate practice, with a focus on children birth to age 3.

The term *developmentally appropriate practice*, or DAP for short, captures a set of core ideas that inform the work of early childhood educators. To gain a thorough understanding of DAP and use it effectively in an infant-toddler program, there is much more to learn and think about than is covered here. As the box on page ix, **Where Did DAP Come From?**, describes, we have detailed the principles and guidelines of developmentally appropriate practice more fully and for children from birth to age 8 in a larger volume (Copple & Bredekamp 2009); a number of other publications address it as well (e.g., Gestwicki 2011; Hart et al. 1997; Kostelnik et al. 1999). In addition, other books also explore developmentally appropriate practice in infant-toddler programs in more detail, which you may want to seek out (e.g., California Department of Education & WestEd Center for Child and Family Studies 2009; Dodge et al. 2010; Post et al. 2011; Zero to Three 2008). As you continue to study and work in the infant-toddler area or in the larger field of early childhood education, you will want to get to know that larger DAP book, as well as some of the many other DAP resources that the National Association for the Education of Young Children (NAEYC), Zero To Three, and similar organizations have produced for teachers, caregivers, administrators, and families.

We offer this book as a first step in your becoming acquainted with the key elements of developmentally appropriate practice, especially as they relate to infants and toddlers. If you are new to the field, or even to this age group, it will introduce you to these core ideas that define this field you are entering. If you have been working with children for some years already, you will find much in this primer that is familiar. We hope it will give you a clearer picture of why you do some of the things you do in the program and why certain of them work better than others. And we hope that you will be able to better communicate with families about what goes on in your program. Whether you are new or experienced, we hope this book will enable you to improve the effectiveness of your work with young children.

What's in this book?

This book is divided into three main parts. The first, **What Is Developmentally Appropriate Practice?**, explains what we mean by DAP and why the decisions that teachers and caregivers make are so important.

Part two, **The Developmentally Appropriate Practitioner**, describes five key aspects of practice that enact DAP principles: creating a caring community of learners, teaching to enhance development and learning, planning appropriate curriculum, assessing children's development and learning, and developing reciprocal relationships with families. Each chapter includes examples and illustrations of developmentally appropriate practice in action.

The third part of the book, **FAQs**, answers the most common inquiries about developmentally appropriate practice we have received from educators, administrators, and parents over the years. They will help you in communicating about its realities and myths and further increase your understanding of the concept, with emphasis on how it applies to infants and toddlers.

Finally, we have included an overview of learning and development for infants and toddlers at different ages, plus references and resources to help guide you on your path to becoming a developmentally appropriate practitioner.

A quick item about vocabulary: In this book the word *teacher* or *caregiver* is used to refer to any adult responsible for a group of children in any program for infants and toddlers, including adults in center-based and family child care and specialists in other disciplines who fulfill the role of caregiver and teacher (e.g., an Early Head Start home visitor). Similarly, the word *program* is intended to imply not only a center setting but any grouping of young children and caregivers, including situations where the focus is parent education.

Basics of Developmentally Appropriate Practice

An Introduction for Teachers of **Infants & Toddlers**

Carol Copple and Sue Bredekamp, with Janet Gonzalez-Mena

National Association for the Education of Young Children
Washington, DC

naeyc ®

National Association for the Education
of Young Children
1313 L Street NW, Suite 500
Washington, DC 20005-4101
202-232-8777 • 800-424-2460
www.naeyc.org

NAEYC Books

Editor in Chief
Akimi Gibson

Editorial Director
Bry Pollack

Senior Editor
Holly Bohart

Design and Production
Malini Dominey

Assistant Editor
Elizabeth Wegner

Editorial Assistant
Ryan Smith

Permissions
Lacy Thompson

Through its publications program, the
National Association for the Education
of Young Children (NAEYC) provides
a forum for discussion of major issues
and ideas in the early childhood field,
with the hope of provoking thought
and promoting professional growth.
The views expressed or implied in this
book are not necessarily those of the
Association or its members.

Cover and inside illustrations by David Clark.
Spot art: p. 16, Natalie Klein; p. 23, Harriet M. Johnson, used by
permission of Bank Street College of Education Publications.

Contributing editor: *Natalie Klein*

Library of Congress Control Number: 2011926728
ISBN: 978-1-928896-73-9
NAEYC Item #324

About the Authors

Carol Copple is a highly respected early childhood education author, educator, and consultant. For 16 years, she directed the books program at NAEYC. She taught at Louisiana State University and the New School for Social Research, and at the Educational Testing Service co-developed and directed a research-based model for preschool education. With Sue Bredekamp, Dr. Copple is co-editor of *Developmentally Appropriate Practice in Early Childhood Programs* (1997; 2009). Among her other books are *Learning to Read and Write: Developmentally Appropriate Practices for Young Children* (NAEYC) and *Educating the Young Thinker: Classroom Strategies for Cognitive Growth* (Erlbaum). She received her doctorate from Cornell University.

Sue Bredekamp is an early childhood education specialist from Washington, DC who serves as a consultant on developmentally appropriate practice, curriculum, teaching, and professional development for state and national organizations such as NAEYC, the Council for Professional Recognition, and Head Start. From 1981 to 1998, she was Director of Accreditation and Professional Development at NAEYC. She is the author of an introductory textbook *Effective Practices in Early Childhood Education: Building a Foundation* (Pearson). Her doctorate is from the University of Maryland.

Janet Gonzalez-Mena has worked with children and families in early childhood education and taught community college. She became interested in infants when she studied with Magda Gerber in the mid-1970s. She is on the faculty for WestEd's Program for Infant-Toddler Caregivers. She has written 15 books and numerous articles. She studied at the Pikler Institute in Budapest where Gerber once studied. Gonzalez-Mena has a master of arts degree in human development from Pacific Oaks College.

Contents

List of Boxes

Where did DAP come from?

That a given activity might be developmentally suited (or not) to children of a particular age level was hardly a novel idea when NAEYC first addressed it. Psychologists and educators had long used the concept. But the need for a more specific description became obvious in the mid-1980s, when NAEYC created a system to accredit early childhood programs. Because the accreditation guidelines required programs to provide "developmentally appropriate experiences" and materials for children, NAEYC needed to give some specifics of what that phrase meant.

Such a description was to be based on what early childhood educators knew about young children through child development theory, research, and practice. NAEYC took the lead in involving the field in considering what practices are developmentally appropriate in working with children of various ages. A position statement on developmentally appropriate practice for preschool children was published in 1986 and expanded in 1987 to cover the full birth to 8-year-old age range.

From the beginning, the description of what was developmentally appropriate was seen as dynamic rather than set in stone—nothing more or less than the best thinking of the field at a particular point in time. Any position statement on DAP would of course be revisited periodically to reflect evolution in the knowledge and thinking of the field.

NAEYC has revised the DAP position statement twice since it first came out, in 1996 and again in 2009. Each revision involved an extensive process of obtaining input from the field. For example, NAEYC invited discussion in conference sessions, online, and through its *Young Children* journal. Further, for both revisions, panels of early childhood leaders met to consider the latest research, issues, and perspectives relating to DAP. NAEYC staff then offered a draft position statement to the field for more comment and refinement. Although some individuals disagree with specific aspects of the statement, most early childhood professionals express general agreement with the basic principles and guidelines of developmentally appropriate practice that NAEYC has articulated.

What Is Developmentally Appropriate Practice?

The Main Idea

Developmentally appropriate practice (DAP) means teaching infants and toddlers in ways that

- **Meet children where they are**, as individuals and as a group
- **Support each child in attaining challenging and achievable goals** that contribute to his or her ongoing development and learning

There's a little more to it than that, but that's the main idea.

For teachers of infants and toddlers, understanding how the youngest children learn and develop is essential. To work with infants, toddlers, and their families, it is important to have a strong foundation in how children from birth through age 3 typically develop. This broad understanding will then help you closely attune to individual children and their families, in all their variety. The more you can know about and tune into the way the children in your group think and learn, the more effective and satisfying your work with them will be. You will gain a clearer sense of direction to guide your actions as you create relationships, set up the environment, and plan curriculum.

Meeting children where they are

Elsewhere in this book, you'll read more about how infants and toddlers learn and how this varies with age and level of development. A broad picture of learning and development and what children are like at different ages, however, is not all you need in order to work with them in a developmentally appropriate way. You won't serve children and families well if you consider only what is "typical" of an age group and if you try to teach and care for children in a one-size-fits-all way. Let's step out of the infant-toddler setting for a moment and visit an everyday scene that illustrates both of these points.

> Coach Todd is a winning soccer coach in a league for girls ages 13–15. He has a good sense of what girls this age enjoy, what they're capable of, and what's usually tough for them, and he has experience in what works in coaching them. Bringing this general knowledge with him on the first day of practice, he knows he won't use the advanced techniques he might with college varsity players, nor will he start out too simply by explaining, "You use your foot to kick the ball." He can make some general plans based on his understanding of what is typical of this age group.
>
> Now, as this season's girls take the field for the first time, Coach Todd watches each one closely and also watches how the team plays together. He gets a feel for each player—her strengths and weaknesses, her temperament, how much experience she has. Based on all this, the coach decides where to start the girls' training, and then keeps watching and making adjustments for each individual player and the team as a whole as the season goes along.

A successful coach like Coach Todd knows he has to meet learners where they are, as individuals and as a group. Pitch the instruction too low and you not only waste learners' time but also show disrespect; pitch it too high and they feel incompetent and frustrated. This is a basic fundamental of any teaching.

Good teachers continually observe children throughout the day during essential daily routines, such as diapering, toileting, eating, hand washing, and resting. They also observe their play. With young babies, observations focus on very simple interactions with available play objects and with caregivers and other babies. The play, of course, becomes more complex as they grow, develop, and learn. Children gradually require much more space to move around in,

more challenging objects to climb on and under, and more complex toys and materials to explore. Their interactions with caregivers and other children also grow more sophisticated. Observation provides information about each child's interests, abilities, and developmental progress.

On the basis of this individualized information, along with general knowledge about the age group, we plan experiences that enhance children's learning and development. Here is what this might look like in an infant group:

> Emily turned over for the first time last week. Today, she is rolling over and over, moving across a small play space with amazing efficiency. Her caregiver, Jamie, watches carefully to see if Emily's rolling will be a problem for the two non-mobile babies sharing her space. It doesn't seem to be. Emily rolls over to Tyler and stops. Tyler looks at her. Emily smiles and then turns to smile at Jamie, who stays close by to make sure nobody gets hurt. She then rolls away from Tyler and happens to see Nadia, who is outside the barricade separating the youngest infants from more mobile babies. Nadia puts a soft toy between the bars of the fence and Emily rolls over to retrieve it. Jamie says, "It looks like you are moving around very well now. Maybe it's almost time to put you out there where you have more room and more toys." Jamie considers both the group's dynamics as well as Emily's developmental progress, and shows respect for Emily by talking directly to her. Her goal is to provide Emily with further experiences to enhance her learning and development by trying her out in a different environment for play and exploration. By closely observing Emily, as well as her peers, Jamie knows just when to transition Emily to join her more mobile friends.

With a group of 30-month-olds, for example, meeting learners where they are might look something like this:

> Mariana notices that Theo has become fascinated with a snail gliding along the gravel in the play area. She gets a piece of dark construction paper and puts the snail on it so Theo can see the slime trail it makes as it moves. She also thinks about getting a glass plate so he can see the snail from underneath. Theo is joined by several other interested toddlers who examine the snail. Mariana decides that tomorrow she'll bring in a picture book on snails.

Or it might look like:

> Because some children in her group understand only a little English, Leila knows she will want to provide nonverbal clues to meaning wherever possible, for example, pictures,

Basics of Developmentally Appropriate Practice

objects, gestures, and demonstrations. She has learned some words in all of the different home languages spoken by the children in her group, and uses them regularly. She also works hard to find volunteers who speak children's home languages. Leila knows that hearing their own language not only helps very young children feel safe and secure, but will also help them to eventually speak English.

Supporting children in attaining challenging and achievable goals

Meeting learners where they are is essential, but no good coach simply *leaves* his players where they are. Coach Todd's aim is always to help each girl improve her soccer skills and understanding as much as she is able, while also making sure she still enjoys the game and wants to continue playing it.

In teaching, these same principles hold. Learners will gain most from experiences or materials that build on what they already know and can do, but they should also be given a chance to stretch a reasonable amount toward what they don't yet know or cannot yet do. For infants and toddlers, these opportunities for growth take place within the context of their relationships.

Developmentally appropriate practice refers to decisions that vary with and adapt to the age, experience, interests, and abilities of individual children within a given age range.

Take the case of picking out books for 2-year-olds. The simple board books younger toddlers enjoy are still appropriate, but now children can start learning to handle books with more care. This in turn allows them access to a greater variety of children's literature. They may still enjoy simple board books, but they are also ready for the challenge of more complex, full-sized picture books as well as the fun of interactive books with moving parts. Because such books introduce new ideas and experiences, they propel children forward and prepare them for more advanced books. Equally important, they will find the just-within-reach books very satisfying and engrossing.

When such a fit exists—that is, when materials or experiences are challenging but not unreasonably beyond the child's ability—we say those materials or experiences are developmentally appropriate for that learner.

✳   ✳   ✳

Here are a few generalizations, then, that can be made about developmentally appropriate practice:

◆ Meet learners where they are, taking into account their physical, emotional, social, and cognitive development and characteristics.

◆ Identify goals for children that are both challenging and achievable—a stretch, but not an impossible leap. During the infant and toddler years, these goals will be especially informed by input from families as well as teacher observation.

◆ Recognize that what makes something challenging and achievable will vary, depending on the individual learner's development in all areas; her store of experiences, knowledge, and skills; and the context within which the learning opportunity takes place.

A cornerstone of developmentally appropriate teaching is *intentionality*. An approach that meets learners where they are and that allows them to reach challenging and achievable goals does not happen by chance. In everything good teachers and caregivers do—from setting up the classroom to observing and assessing children to planning the curriculum—they are intentional. They are purposeful and thoughtful about the actions they take, and they base their actions on the outcomes that the program and children's families are trying to help children reach. Even when responding to unexpected opportunities—"teachable moments"—the intentional teacher is guided by those desired outcomes.

An intentional teacher has clearly defined learning and developmental goals for children, which are informed by direct observation, input from families, and knowledge of child development. Together with families, intentional teachers thoughtfully choose strategies that will enable infants and toddlers to achieve these goals; teachers also continually assess children's progress toward those goals and adjust strategies used to reach them. Having their goals and plans in mind for each child, intentional teachers are well prepared to discuss with others—parents, administrators, colleagues—what they are doing. Not only do they know what to do, they also know why they are doing it and can describe that rationale.

Embracing infants and toddlers within the context of family-based relationships

Each infant or toddler entering a program comes from a home context. Bronfenbrenner (1979) developed a whole theory about the child and the systems that impact the child, the most important being home and family. The people the child lives with have great influence on the child, and they in turn are influenced by a number of forces, including culture, history, background, where they live, beliefs, experiences, and so much more. When infants and toddlers start a program, the only way to meet those children where they are is to learn about where they've come from. We must build a relationship with the family while also building a relationship with their child.

> Ten-month-old Makayla is new to her program. She clings to her mother and resists being put down. Even though she has visited several times, she still resists being left without her mother. Fortunately for her, both her mother and her caregiver are supportive of her feelings and project confidence, secure in the knowledge that she will adjust.

Intentional teachers relate to parents, and can learn some ways from them to make their children comfortable in an out-of-home setting.

Infants and toddlers only learn within the context of relationships, and they learn best when they feel secure. Building attachments is a primary road to security (Honig 2002). That's why it's a positive sign when a baby or toddler cries at the beginning when her parent leaves; it's a sign that she's attached to the parent. Though separation anxiety may be hard on parents—and maybe also on caregivers—it's still a good sign. The goal in an infant-toddler program is not to lessen attachment to family members; it is to maintain it while simultaneously building attachments with a particular caregiver or caregivers in that program. Firm attachment, plus feelings of security and trust, provides the foundations of learning for infants and toddlers.

Deciding What Is Developmentally Appropriate

Teachers and caregivers who are committed to developmentally appropriate practice enact that commitment in the decisions they make about the environment, interactions, curriculum, and teaching. To make good decisions they must know a lot about the infants and toddlers in their group, and about their families. Where *are* those children in their learning and development? Individually, or in relation to others? Which goals will be challenging and achievable for them, and which would be an unreasonable stretch?

Three fundamental considerations should guide us in our information gathering and decision making:

1. **Consider what is age appropriate—that is, based on what we know about the development and learning of children within a given age range.**

Infants and toddlers think and play and feel and see the world in ways that are different from the way that older children or adults do, and these ways change as they develop and

Think about the difference between a 46-year-old and a 48-year-old. You probably couldn't tell which was which. Not so with children. Now think about the vast difference between a newborn and a 1-year-old and a 2-year-old. What a difference a year can make! For the very young, even a month or a week typically brings big changes.

learn. Age is a significant predictor of a child's characteristics, abilities, and understandings. Knowing about these age-related characteristics, though only a starting point, is vital for early childhood teachers to be effective. (The charts in **A Changing Picture: Children at 0–9 Months, 8–18 Months, and 16–36 Months,** beginning on page 81, summarize the abilities and behaviors common among infants and toddlers of different ages and stages.)

Caregivers and teachers who know a lot about children's development are able to make broad predictions about what the children in an age group will be like and what will benefit them. This knowledge enables us to make some preliminary decisions and be fairly confident that our plans will be an appropriate starting point for that group. For example,

> Erika has three infants in her group, two of whom are quite active. One crawls and climbs; the other has learned to walk. She knows that the third baby, who is just turning over, needs her own protected space to move freely and safely without intrusion from the more active infants. Erika sets up a safe area on the floor for that child, and creates a more challenging environment for the other two with things to crawl under, over, and through.

> Shantal has 2- to 3-year-olds in her class, and enjoys choosing art materials for the children to explore and experiment with. Today, she covers a small table with paper and offers cups of crayons arranged by color. The children are working on what could be considered a joint project, talking to each other as they draw. Mostly they freely explore and experience the sensations in their arms and hands while observing how the crayons mark the paper. They don't seem to be drawing anything in particular, though one 3-year-old tells Shantal his round marks are pancakes.

So, age matters—it gets us started in gauging what approaches and experiences will be most effective for children in a particular age range. At the same time, good teachers and caregivers recognize that each individual and group is different. Averages and norms never tell the whole story, do they? There are always significant individual differences, which brings us to the second dimension.

2. Consider what is individually appropriate—that is, attuned to each child in all of his or her individuality.

Effective teachers get to know the individual children in a group and observe them closely. From those observations we can make more specific plans and

Special challenges in mixed-age groups of infants and toddlers

Children aren't born in litters (with rare exceptions), so parents who have more than one child are raising them in mixed-aged groups. Family child care providers and even some center-based programs also often have mixed-age groups. Although it may be challenging to plan a developmentally appropriate program under those circumstances, it's not impossible.

For example, setting up a safe, interesting, and educational environment for babies who are not yet mobile takes some thought when there are also babies present who crawl and toddlers who can walk, run, and even climb. Developmental appropriateness is important and always goes hand in hand with safety. Children of all ages (except those in the first weeks of life) need freedom to move and space to explore. At the same time, the ones who aren't yet mobile need protection from the ones who are. Babies and toddlers also need different play objects in the environment.

Along with the challenges of mixed-age groups come benefits, as well. Older children can serve as role models for the younger ones. Cross-age friendships are another benefit.

adjustments to accommodate those children's varying rates of development within and across various developmental areas. Some 18-month-olds, for example, can already do some things more typical of 24-month-olds, while a few 24-month-olds aren't yet doing these things. Moreover, any one child's development will be uneven across different developmental areas.

> Among the children in Shantal's class, Maxwell is more advanced in his gross motor skills than he is socially or cognitively. José has well-developed language skills but has less ability at certain gross motor skills such as walking up and down stairs.

In addition to their developmental differences, children also differ in many other respects—their likes and dislikes, personalities and learning styles, knowledge and skills based on prior experiences, and more. Responding to each child's individual needs and abilities is fundamental to developmentally appropriate practice and certainly applies to children with special learning and developmental needs as well as to more typically developing children. Good teaching and caregiving can never be the same for all. It always requires us meeting each learner where he or she is and tailoring that developing learner's goals so they are always challenging and achievable.

> As Shantal makes plans to help all the children make significant progress in their language development, she has some overall strategies for the group. Beyond these, she has different plans and strategies in mind for the child who is not yet speaking, the child who is a dual-language learner, the verbal child with a large vocabulary, and so on.

3. Consider what is appropriate to the social and cultural contexts in which children live.

All of us growing up, first as members of our particular family and later as members of a broader social and cultural community, come to certain understandings about what our groups consider appropriate, valued, expected, and admired. We learn this through direct teaching from our parents and other important people in our lives and through observing and modeling the behavior of those around us. Among these understandings we learn "rules" about how to show respect, how to interact with people we know well and those we have just met, how to regard time and personal space, how to dress, and countless other behaviors we perform every day. We typically learn the rules very early and very deeply, so we live by them with little conscious thought.

For the young children in our programs, what makes sense to them and what they are able to learn and respond to depend on the social and cultural contexts to which they are accustomed. Responsive teachers and caregivers take such contextual factors into account, along with the children's ages and their purely individual differences, in shaping all aspects of the learning environment.

Culture is the socially transmitted behaviors, attitudes, and values shared by a group.

Some infants and toddlers have had little experience in moving between cultures. Those who have lived entirely in the familiar confines of home and neighborhood find venturing into the new world of the program setting a very big change. For those children whose language or social and cultural background differs from that predominating in the program, the situation is more drastic. Too often they find very little that is familiar in this new place, and much that is scary and confusing.

It is the teacher's job to take the children's social and cultural experiences into account in planning the daily environment and learning experiences. As Marulis writes about her classroom:

> [The goal] is creating an environment that says "everyone is welcome here. . . ." In my classroom, there is not one way of seeing, hearing, touching, tasting, or feeling things. (2000)

Figuring out how to create an environment that says "everyone is welcome here" means discovering the components that make infants and toddlers feel safe, comfortable, and at home. Hearing their own language is important, and discovering connections between the way things are done in the program and the way they are done at home provides comfort. Familiar food is important, too. Welcoming infants and toddlers to a program means communicating with families to understand social and cultural differences.

Being responsive to social and cultural differences can be quite a challenge. Our own culture is so integral to who we are, so much a part of our daily experience of the world, that, like breathing, we may not even be aware of it. If ours is the predominant culture or if we are in a position of power, as a teacher is, it can be easy to ignore or devalue cultures different from ours. Even if we are aware of our own culture and respectful of others around us, we still can forget how much harder it is for young children to make the shifts that negotiating different social and cultural contexts requires. This holds true even when children's families are adept at being bicultural.

Early childhood teachers and caregivers have several responsibilities in this regard. First, we must take care not to make judgments about children's behavior without taking the children's (and our own) social and cultural contexts into account. Let's look at an example.

> Although many Europeans and Americans of European descent expect children to make eye contact with them, children from many Latin American and Asian cultures show respect by avoiding the gaze of authority figures. Sharon is unfamiliar with this difference in cultural norms, and using her personal cultural lens, she interprets 3-year-old Haru's lack of eye contact as shyness at best and a sign of disrespect at worst. Sometimes she thinks

Developmentally appropriate shopping

To keep in mind the three kinds of knowledge that should inform our decisions about practice, let's take a developmentally appropriate shopping trip.

Suppose you are shopping for a dress for your 8-year-old goddaughter to wear to a school musical performance. Taking age as a starting point, you'll likely start in the "Girls 7–10" department. You figure that will be the right ballpark—the clothes fitting most girls in the 7–10 age range. This dimension is considering **age appropriateness** in decision making.

Now that you're in the right department, will you just pull any size 8 dress off the rack and take it to the register? No, there's more to consider. Let's say your goddaughter is petite in comparison with her peers.

You've seen that she tends to look good in certain styles, and you know she hates pink. These preferences and characteristics will further direct your search. This dimension is considering **individual appropriateness** in decision making.

Finally, you take into account her peer group and family background. Although she may be looking for an outfit her favorite pop idol would wear, you know it wouldn't be appropriate for a school performance. And because you know that the cultural background of your goddaughter's family disposes them to dressing up for such occasions, you steer in that direction in making a choice. Weighing such knowledge is taking account of **social and cultural contexts**.

---

it's just inattention, and treats the child accordingly. Other times, she suspects it could be development delays.

When a teacher's cultural blinders lead her to draw wrong conclusions, as Sharon did about Haru's lack of eye contact, she is unable to provide a developmentally appropriate learning environment for the child.

Further, teachers must be able to forge the cultural bridges that young children need to thrive in the early childhood setting.

When Michael first offers Kendra finger food, as he does with the rest of the toddlers at his center, Kendra seems very hesitant about touching it. Then Michael finds out that in Kendra's family culture, no one ever picks up food with their hands, no matter how young they are. Kendra's grandmother is very firm when she says that they want for Kendra to continue to always use a fork or a spoon at the center. Michael is faced with a challenge, but he wants to be culturally responsive, so he assures Kendra's grandmother that he will go along with what the family wants. He works with the kitchen staff to figure out how to serve snacks that can be eaten with utensils, and he always provides Kendra with a fork and spoon. He watches with pleasure at how well she is able to use them.

The responsibility for learning about children's social and cultural contexts lies with the teacher. You can become more familiar with the social and cultural contexts of the children in your group in a variety of ways, including talking with families, visiting children's homes, and enlisting the help of community volunteers familiar with children's home cultures. Additional suggestions and detail are provided in various publications in the **Resources** list. (More about working with families comes in part two of this book.)

✳   ✳   ✳

To recap, when working with children, an effective teacher begins by thinking about what children of a given age and developmental level are like. This knowledge provides a general idea of the activities, routines, interactions, and curriculum that will be effective with them. But the teacher also has to look at children within the context of their family, community, culture, social group, past experience, and current circumstances, and she must consider each child as an individual. Only then can she make decisions that are developmentally appropriate—that is, age appropriate, individually appropriate, and culturally appropriate.

How Young Children Learn and Develop

Transporting the full set of teaching methods used with college students, middle schoolers, or even third-graders to the early childhood setting—and especially to an infant-toddler group—would be a dismal failure. But if very young children learn best in certain ways, what are these? Infants and toddlers learn through the following:

Relationships with responsive adults. In the early years of life, relationships with nurturing, responsive adults are essential as the building blocks of healthy development (Shonkoff & Phillips 2000). Relationships as the context for learning and development are vitally important in the infant and toddler years.

> Relationships provide the framework for infant development. When relationships are . . . responsive and reciprocal, they help children break down the incoming stream of information from the outside world so that they can assimilate and understand it, while also providing predictable responses so children can trust it. (Raikes & Edwards 2009, 2)

Positive teacher-child relationships promote not only children's social competence and emotional development but also their academic learning (Pianta 2000). In infant and toddler programs, it's crucial to have one or two *primary caregivers,* who create special relationships with each child in their care (Lally 1995).

Caregivers may have several children as their "primaries." Also important is *continuity of care,* which means that the child stays with the same primary caregiver in the same peer group over many months—from year to year, if possible. Continuity of care is especially important for infants, as they need it to ensure that they (and their parents!) can form attachments to the one or two primary caregivers. Providing continuity from year to year is logistically more difficult, but it can still be achieved through various means such as mixed-age groups or "looping" (where the adult moves with a group of children to a new room as they grow and develop [Baker & Manfredi/Petitt 2004]).

Active, hands-on involvement. Young children learn best when they are actively involved. As they play, explore, experiment, and interact with people and objects, children are always trying to make sense of those experiences. Children under age 3 are most comfortable in the concrete, sensory world they see, smell, hear, taste, and touch.

Although hands-on learning opportunities suit infants and toddlers to a tee, equally important is for experiences to also be "mind-on," that is, to engage children's thinking processes and encourage them to investigate, question, and ponder problems. At first, problem solving is purely physical, but it isn't long before the mind also becomes engaged.

Meaningful experiences. We all learn best when information and concepts are meaningful to us, that is, connected to what we already know and understand. Although true for people of all ages, this fact about learning is even truer for very young children. Children learn best when they can relate new knowledge to what they have already encountered, to what is already important to them. Then they can weave new threads into the fabric of their previous knowledge and experiences. For example, books about babies or new siblings are likely to be of interest to 2-year-olds who have younger siblings or are in a program where they see babies.

Constructing their understanding of the world. Young children are mentally active learners who are always "constructing" their knowledge or understanding of the world. That is, they are continually working to figure things out on their own terms. The younger the child, the more this is done physically. The first years of life are all about trying to make sense of the world around them. As Gopnik says, "When they play, children actively experiment on the world and they use the results of those experiments to change what they think" (2009, 244).

Even learning what a word refers to, which may sound straightforward, involves the child sorting out what that word does and doesn't include. As children engage in this process of construction, they often come up with ideas that are quite different from what adults *think* they have conveyed.

> Marcus, a 2-year-old, on several occasions hears his family members refer to his soft yellow ball with the word *ball* ("Ball, Marcus, here's your ball"). So Marcus learns that this particular object is "ball." But if he is to generalize the word appropriately to other objects in the world, he has some figuring out to do. Maybe his parents are referring to the bright yellow color, and so any yellow thing is a ball? Or could it be anything you throw? Or is a ball anything of rounded shape, like the kitchen clock? Marcus may reach toward an orange, a balloon, or a round light fixture, saying "Ball!" And the idea that something oblong like a football could also be a ball may never occur to him.

Eventually, through many, many experiences with *ball,* the child will hone in on a concept that matches the same one adults mean when they use that term. But this does not occur overnight—there is construction to be done. Children keep putting the bits and pieces together, trying to relate them and make sense of them.

As children play, they are actively constructing meaning. For this reason, observing play can be a window into their understandings and concerns.

> Two-year-old Aidan keeps asking for band-aids for his baby doll's "owie." Amy offers some masking tape, which Aidan puts on the doll. He turns to Amy and says, "All better now!" Amy knows that Aidan's mother gave birth a week ago and that his new sister is still in the hospital. Aidan doesn't know what's wrong with her, but he can use what he does know to play out some of his feelings about what he has been told.

Play is a powerful way that children work through and try to make sense of the happenings and routines in their daily lives, which they don't entirely understand but want very much to process and take control of.

What good is play?

A milestone in infant play comes when children discover their hands and start exploring what they can do. The look on their faces and the intense interest they show tell us how valuable play is even at this tender age. Play advances as infants explore their environment and the objects and people in it. They discover how things work. Between the ages of 2 and 3, play becomes more complex and imaginative. The benefits of play are numerous!

In play, children make choices, solve problems, converse, and negotiate. They create make-believe events and practice physical, social, and cognitive skills. As they play, children are able to express and work out emotional aspects of everyday experiences and events they find disturbing. Through playing together and taking on different roles, children also grow in their ability to see something from another person's point of view and to engage in leading and following behaviors—both of which they will need to get along well as adults (Sawyers & Rogers 1988). In all these ways, play can be a milieu unsurpassed in promoting children's development and learning.

Although we think of play as the essence of freedom and spontaneity, it is also the time when children are most motivated to regulate their own behavior according to certain "musts"—restrictions they put on themselves about what they can say and do because the play demands it (Bodrova & Leong 2003). They know that to stay in the play, which they very much want to do, they must follow its rules. And children monitor each other pretty closely to make sure that everyone does just that ("Sammy, you're supposed to be the daddy—daddies don't bark!"). In their pretending, children take care to follow these rules, adapting their physical actions and speech as needed—walking heavily to play an elephant, talking in a high, babyish voice to portray an infant, staying in role—and in this process they become more capable of self-regulation (Vygotsky 1934/1986).

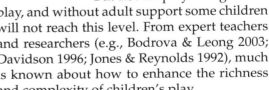

In interactive play, as compared with more structured activities, children tend to exhibit higher language levels, more innovation and problem solving, greater empathy and cooperation, and longer attention spans (Smilansky 1990). So it's not surprising that young children's engagement in high-level play is one of the best predictors of later school success (Smilansky 1990).

But not all play is high-level play, and without adult support some children will not reach this level. From expert teachers and researchers (e.g., Bodrova & Leong 2003; Davidson 1996; Jones & Reynolds 1992), much is known about how to enhance the richness and complexity of children's play.

*　　*　　*

As important as it is to recognize the active construction children engage in, this does not mean they have no need for adults to convey information and further their learning. Children certainly don't need to discover or work out *everything* for themselves—how inefficient, indeed impossible, that would be! They need adults to teach them many things. Some of these things are most efficiently imparted directly; for example, telling a child climbing up on a chair that "Feet belong on the floor." Other understandings involve a great deal of experience and construction on the child's part.

There are in fact many ways that we can promote very young children's learning and development. In the course of every day, caregivers and teachers must draw on a wide range of teaching strategies. We look at some of those strategies later, in the chapter **Teach to Enhance Development and Learning.**

The Developmentally
Appropriate Practitioner

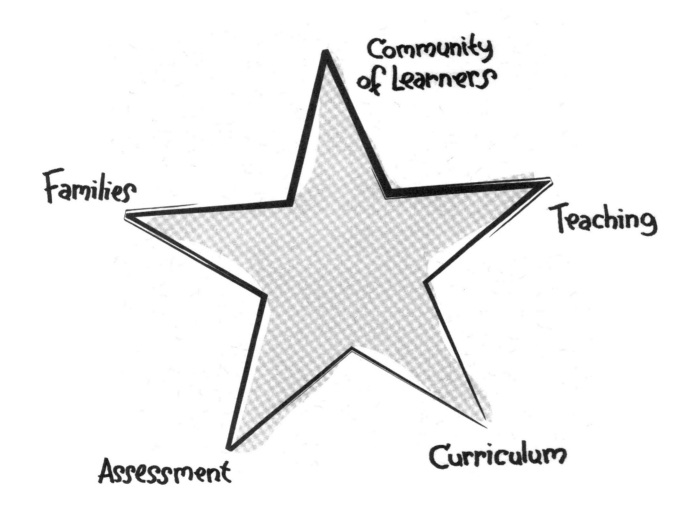

Community
of Learners

Families

Teaching

Assessment

Curriculum

Guidelines for Developmentally Appropriate Practice

In part one we described what developmentally appropriate practice is: That it is based on knowledge of how young children develop and learn. And that it results from the process of teachers making decisions about the well-being and education of children based on what is age appropriate, individually appropriate, and appropriate to children's social and cultural contexts.

From such understanding flow guidelines to inform the practice of all early childhood teachers. That is, what teachers must *do* to enact DAP principles. Those guidelines define five key aspects of good teaching:

1. **Creating a caring community of learners**
2. **Teaching to enhance development and learning**
3. **Planning appropriate curriculum**
4. **Assessing children's development and learning**
5. **Developing reciprocal relationships with families**

These five aspects of teachers' work are closely interrelated. A good mental model to keep them in mind is a five-pointed star. Each point of the star represents one vital part of what teachers and infant-toddler programs do to achieve key goals for children. None can be left out or shortchanged without seriously weakening the whole. Now let's look at each in turn.

1. Create a Caring Community of Learners

The developmentally appropriate program is a place where infants and toddlers experience nurturing relationships, feel part of something positive, and where the stage is set for children to grow into responsible members of a democratic society. Children learn and develop best when they are part of a community of learners—a group in which all participants are growing in their ability to consider and contribute to one another's well-being and learning.

Teachers of toddlers can see the roots of this community form as children start learning about others' feelings, but can an infant group really be seen as a true community? The answer is yes, if we delve a bit deeper into what a "community" is made of. Relationships based on strong bonds of affection and agreement are at the core of any community (Etzioni 1996), and the ability to form these types of relationships starts with the bonds children form with their special people in infancy.

To create such a group, teachers and caregivers must

◆ Be empathic observers and respond in meaningful ways to what they believe the infant or toddler is trying to understand or accomplish

◆ Get to know each child's personality, abilities, and ways of learning

- Make sure that all children get the support they need to develop relationships with their families, caregivers, and peers within the group structure
- Work to build a strong sense of group affinity among the children—to develop a sense of group connection
- Create an environment that is organized, orderly, and comfortable for children
- Plan ways for children to occasionally work and play collaboratively with peers or adults
- Bring each child's home culture and language into the shared culture of the group
- Discourage unsociable practices that exclude some children and undermine a sense of community, making them feel like outsiders

In a caring community of learners, everyone feels...

I belong here.
I am safe.
I matter, and everyone else in the group matters too.
When we have problems we can work them out.
Together we can do great things.

The classroom community is inclusive

In a developmentally appropriate program, children with special learning needs are included as full participants in the social and learning environment. Program staff use the necessary supports and strategies to ensure that each child's individual needs are met. Researchers, teachers, and parents report that children with and without disabilities benefit in many ways from inclusive programs (Odom et al. 2002; Ong & Cole 2009). When we work to ensure that the children with special needs are truly included in all aspects of the program, not only these children benefit but all the children in the group gain in understanding and acceptance of the differences among people.

Physical environment and schedule

In establishing the kind of environment and community in which infants and toddlers can thrive, teachers give thoughtful consideration to the physical environment well before the first day and from then on. For infants and toddlers, the term "schedule" has a different meaning than for older children. For the most part, young infants are on their own body schedule. By the time they are older toddlers, routines such as eating and sleeping will become more predictable and in sync with other children their age.

Ensure children's health and safety. The classroom environment reflects the program's goals—at the most basic level, that children be healthy and safe. Toward this end, all program staff work together to make sure that the indoor and outdoor environments meet health and safety standards. Accessibility for children or family members with physical disabilities is also important. (See **Resources** for some publications and websites that can help you address safety issues.)

Keep classrooms lively and "explorable." Beyond being a safe place, the developmentally appropriate environment continually invites children's initiative and active exploration of materials. Materials are well organized and physically within reach to enable children to readily find and use them. Effective teachers and caregivers create a rich learning environment that changes often enough to be fresh and interesting to children and yet remains consistent enough to be predictable and understandable to them. Young children need to know what's available and where. But they lose interest when they find all the same materials in the environment day after day.

Take into account evolving learning needs. Children's interests, development, and learning needs also evolve over the course of the year. Over time they are ready for greater complexity and challenge than they were on first entering the program. With an eye to holding children's interest and helping them move forward in all areas, teachers change materials periodically, keeping enough of the same to promote a sense of security in infants and toddlers who depend on predictability. Also, effective caregivers pay attention to the toys and materials that certain children seek out regularly. Here are some examples of ways attuned adults might change the environment. For example, over time teachers might provide toddlers with more challenging puzzles featuring a greater number of pieces. At the water table, they might introduce new problems and stimulate new investigations by replacing children's usual materials with items that leak, such as colanders, funnels, and eye droppers.

Carefully plan daily routines. Hand in hand with an organized physical environment is a well-thought-out daily routine. Infants and toddlers need predictability, and a consistent schedule helps them develop their sense of time and sequence. Infants need individualized schedules that meet their personal needs for eating, changing, rest, and exploration. Infants and toddlers also need a general sense of what will happen next. The schedule needs to be fairly predictable, but not rigid. Teachers and caregivers plan for balance in the children's day: times for rest and times for vigorous activity; time outdoors as well as indoors; times to do things together in pairs or small groups and times to work independently (more in a later chapter on effectively using different learning contexts).

Guidance in a caring community

How we interact with children shapes how they approach others, how they feel about themselves, and how they develop and learn. We are models; we must keep in mind that children naturally pick up how we behave and will imitate us. If we don't want them to yell at each other, we must also not yell. Our expectations for their behavior affect them too. If we expect them to behave badly, they generally will. If we expect them to make good choices and treat others respectfully, more often than not they will do that.

Guiding young children's behavior begins with building a warm, positive relationship with them. Also crucial is organizing the environment and schedule so children can do their best (e.g., not rushing an activity, not introducing new challenges at the end of the day when children can be tired and cranky), and making learning experiences engaging and appropriate for them so they won't be bored or unduly frustrated.

Self-regulation is the ability to focus attention and manage one's emotions and behaviors according to the demands of the situation. The self-regulatory abilities that children gradually develop—or fail to develop—powerfully affect their interaction with people around them and influence their learning and eventual school success.

Of course, guidance with young infants is a different story—it isn't until an infant becomes mobile that what we usually think of as guidance begins. However, when the environment is completely safe and appropriate, there isn't much an infant can do that's unacceptable except be rough with another child. In that case, the best approach is to model gentleness.

Finally, responsive teachers use every opportunity—and make opportunities, as well—to teach children social skills and help them develop self-regulation. In the early childhood years, guidance isn't something we do so we "can get on with the curriculum." Instead, positive social and emotional development are themselves key curricular goals for children.

Developmentally appropriate guidance shows respect for children. It helps them understand and grow, rather than punishing or shaming them. It is directed toward helping children develop self-regulation and the ability to make better decisions in the future. Teachers are using effective guidance when they

◆ Value mistakes as learning opportunities

◆ Listen and promptly respond when babies cry and when toddlers talk about their feelings and frustrations

◆ Guide toddlers to resolve conflicts, and model for children the skills they need to solve problems on their own

◆ Set limits and patiently remind toddlers of those limits and the rationales behind them

When teachers work to give children a solid foundation in their emotional development and ability to relate well to others, children carry that foundation with them into their future lives in and out of school.

2. Teach to Enhance Development and Learning

Whatever infant-toddler setting or age group you work with, you are responsible for actively supporting children's development and learning. There is no magic formula for doing this. Good infant-toddler professionals continually use their knowledge and judgment to make decisions about the environment, materials, interactions, and learning experiences likely to be most effective for the group and each individual in it.

When working with infants and young toddlers, avoid interpreting the word *teach* as instruction based on showing or explaining how to do something. That is a minimal part of teaching infants and toddlers. Obviously, *teach* is used in a more general sense in this book, but even in its broadest sense, *teaching* toddlers—and especially infants—can never be a one-way process.

As Elizabeth Jones notes, working with very young children is a "teaching/ learning process" (1978). Likewise, infant specialist Magda Gerber often emphasized that "The baby is the teacher!" (Hammond 2009). The teacher is also the learner. Only when you learn who the baby is and what that baby needs, wants, or is ready for at any given time can you assume the role of teacher in its broadest sense. You must learn how to respond to meet children's needs and support their development and learning. This may be through particular interactions, or perhaps through materials provided in the environment. It is also key to infuse language into interactions by using words to explain what you perceive from the baby and what you will do in response.

Sometimes debates on practices can get cast as "either/or" choices. For example, one side shouts, "Teach those babies!" and the other retorts, "Only child-initiated learning works!" But if we all step back a bit, we can usually see that *both* approaches have some value and a place in the program—it is a matter of "both/and" rather than "either/or." So it is with using teaching/learning strategies.

Using a wide range of teaching/learning strategies— the teacher's tool belt

As we think about multiple strategies for teaching and interacting with very young children, consider as an analogy the constructing of a table or repairing of a roof. No skilled carpenter tries to do every part of his work with the same tool. He doesn't use a screwdriver to drive a nail into a board or a hammer to twist in a screw.

Like a competent carpenter, a good teacher has many tools, or teaching/learning strategies, in her tool belt. She selects the best strategy to use at any given moment, depending on the learning goal, specific situation, and needs of the child. That is, the adult is choosing the strategy she thinks will be most useful in a particular situation. Often she may try one strategy, see that it doesn't work, and try something else. What's important is to have a variety of strategies at the ready and to remain flexible and observant.

Below are descriptions of teaching strategies that are key to the effective teacher's repertoire. Certainly others exist, and there are many variations. Moreover, strategies often are used in combination; in a single sentence, for example, a professional might both *acknowledge* a child's actions and *give her a cue or challenge* ("Mara, you found the ball you were looking for. But it's under the table. I wonder what you can do now?"). We should also point out that the terms for the strategies we use below are not universal. Various infant-toddler models and programs have their own special labels for what teachers do. Our purpose is simply to look at several major kinds of strategies that teachers and caregivers need to have at their disposal to do their job well:

Acknowledge: Give positive attention that tells the child you noticed what he said or did (*e.g., responding to babbling with eye contact and a gentle touch or a sound in response; saying thank you when a child picks up something you dropped*).

Encourage: Offer comments or nonverbal actions that promote the child's persistence and effort (*"You really worked hard at getting that toy untangled, James"*), rather than giving the child evaluative praise (*"Good job, James"*).

Give specific feedback: Offer specific rather than general comment on the child's performance (*"I wonder what would happen if you tried using the spoon instead of the fork to eat the apple sauce"*).

Model: Display for children a skill or desirable way of behaving (*whispering when you want children to lower their own voices; modeling cooperation and problem solving by saying, "You both want the shovel—what can we do? Maybe we can look for another shovel"*).

Demonstrate: Show the correct way to perform a procedure that needs to be done in a certain way (*e.g., how to wash one's hands thoroughly or put a tissue in the wastebasket*).

Create or add challenge: Generate a problem or add difficulty to a task or step so that it is a bit beyond what children have already mastered (*e.g., ask toddlers to predict whether a toy will sink or float, and then let them test it out*).

Give a cue, hint, or other assistance: Help children to work "on the edge" of their current competence (*e.g., offering suggestions to two toddlers struggling over a toy then waiting to see if they can work through the conflict on their own before intervening*).

Provide information: Directly give children facts (*"Birds make nests like this one to live in"*), verbal labels (*"This is a cup"*), and other information.

Give directions: Provide specific instructions for children's action or behavior (*"Put the block on the shelf next to the other blocks"; "Let's use our hands so gently"*).

With some of these strategies, children receive new information or directions, and in others they are spurred to think and solve problems. Some strategies give children feedback to improve. Some simply encourage them to persist in tackling a problem or working on a skill they haven't yet mastered. Teaching/learning strategies differ in their uses and the demands they place on the child, but all can be valid and useful, depending on the goal and situation. An intentional teacher will be able not only to choose which strategy will suit a certain situation but also to describe why she chose that specific strategy.

In this example, the teacher has her tool kit ready, and makes use of various strategies as needed:

Beth teaches 2-year-olds in a center-based program. Early in the year, she observes that the children are fascinated with vehicles, but they do little more than run in circles making siren sounds. Their play lacks focus and conversation, and it often breaks down into chaos. She wants to introduce the children to other possibilities and help them to play at a higher level.

One day, when Anna, Casey, and Tyrell are running around, Beth decides to join their play. She sets up four chairs in a row, announces that the chairs are a bus, and **models** the role of the bus driver. "We're going on a trip today. Who wants to come?"

The children quickly become interested and Beth helps them into the seats. Beth sits in the first chair. "Let's sing 'The Wheels on the Bus!'" she suggests, in order to foster their oral language skills. The group begins to sing, with Beth occasionally pausing before a repeated phrase to let the children fill it in. The children sing out the missing words with glee.

"Wait a minute!" she exclaims. "We forgot to bring the babies on the bus! Should we get them?" The children start shouting their agreement, and Beth says, "Let's go get them from the shelf with our babies." She **creates a challenge**—one she knows will vary with the individual child—by asking, "See if you can each get a baby to bring, but be very quiet and hold them carefully. They're all asleep!"

The children scoop up the baby dolls. Casey grabs three babies, but can't hold them all. Beth **gives assistance** by picking the dolls up and suggesting he take just one, and then putting the two extra dolls back. For Anna, she **demonstrates** how to carefully hold a baby. For Tyrell, who has greater motor control, she **adds more challenge.** "Tyrell, see if you can walk really quietly back to the bus while holding your baby." As the children settle back into their chairs, Beth **acknowledges** and **encourages** their efforts. "You all are so careful with your babies," she tells the children. "I know you can hold them gently so they'll be comfortable."

When everyone is seated, Beth adds some use of pattern—an aspect of mathematics—to the learning experience. She chants, *"Let's . . . go . . . drive the bus! Let's . . . go . . . drive the bus!"* in a marching rhythm, while creating a steady beat by slapping her hand against her leg. After several repetitions, the children are chanting along with her patterned phrase. This continues for a few minutes, ending as Beth leads the children in a chorus of "Hooray!" Beth says to the children, "We took a long trip today and had fun. Who came on our trip?" Tyrell jumps up and says "Me! Me!" while Anna waves her baby. Casey says "Casey and Ms. Beth and babies!" Beth **provides information** when she says, "Yes, we all went on the trip. Buses are big, and can fit a lot of people!"

This vignette illustrates how the full range of teaching strategies may be used in any context. Although play is an open-ended activity, the teacher may directly provide information or create challenges in the play setting. Likewise, when working with small groups, the teacher may ask questions and use other techniques to engage the children in problem solving or generating ideas.

Scaffolding children's learning

In the first chapter we saw that developmentally appropriate goals are both challenging and achievable. The most effective learning experiences build on what children already know and can do, but also get them to stretch a reasonable amount toward what the children don't yet know or cannot yet do. That's why the phrase "teaching/learning strategies" makes sense. We must learn what each infant or toddler knows and can do and figure out what's needed to help them grow, develop, and learn.

But learners cannot spend all their time stretched "on their tiptoes." They also need plenty of opportunity to practice the skills they are in the process of acquiring. They need to feel solid mastery and a sense of being successful. Children should not just be rushed on to the next challenge; they need a sense of the goal having been achieved. Once children have mastered a skill or concept, they are ready for the next stretch.

Then, as a child begins a new challenge, he may need some support from the teacher to enable him to manage it. At the same time, a skilled teacher doesn't overdo the help. The aim is to provide the least amount of support that the child needs to do something he cannot quite do on his own. For example, if a child trying to place a puzzle piece is getting increasingly frustrated and about to give up, she might say, "What happens if you turn that piece?" She offers the least help necessary, and then sits back and lets the child continue on his own. If the teacher had placed the puzzle piece for him instead, he would be less likely to learn to do it himself.

As the child begins to master the new skill or acquire the new understanding, the teacher gradually reduces the support provided. Soon the child who has been receiving assistance will be able to handle the skill or task without support. Because the teacher provides the support only as long as it is needed, providing support in this way is called *scaffolding*—like the temporary structures that builders or painters stand on to get to spots high up on a house they couldn't otherwise reach.

Teachers and caregivers use scaffolding to help children make progress in all areas of learning and development throughout the day. The scaffolding can take many forms, using any of the strategies listed on page 38. For example, you could

◆ Ask a question or give another sort of hint to alert the child to some aspect of the task that has been missed (e.g., "Does the cup go on the chair or on the table?")

◆ Ask an infant to lift her bottom when you are diapering. If she doesn't understand or respond, lift her bottom to show what you mean, and the next time she might lift it on her own

◆ Pair a toddler with another toddler who has complementary strengths— they will be able to do things together that neither initially could do alone

Using a variety of contexts for learning and development

Besides being intentional about the strategies they use, the support they provide, or other teaching interactions, effective caregivers and teachers think carefully about the learning context or format that is best for helping children achieve a desired outcome. The three major kinds of learning formats for infants and toddlers are groups, play environments, and routines. Each has its own characteristics, functions, and value.

It should be noted that a whole-group format is usually not appropriate for children birth to age 3. There are times when the whole group is together, such as meal times for toddlers, but usually children are playing or being cared for in smaller groups, pairs, or individually. Though there may be something the teacher wants to make sure *all* the children share, it is not natural for infants and toddlers to participate in a large group and pay attention for periods of time. Very young children learn through play—moving, exploring, and experimenting. When the whole group is together for some reason, the most important principle is to read the children's cues and not keep going after they start to lose interest.

Small groups. Interactions with infants are nearly always individual, but adults can engage with children between ages 18 and 36 months in pairs or small groups. Caregivers and teachers often use this format when they are introducing a new experience or object and particularly want to encourage some interaction among toddlers. For example, Kelly brought a drum to the toddler room—large enough for several children to gather around. She brought two or three children over at a time to explore the sounds they could make with their hands and other objects.

Small groups vary in size, usually consisting of three or four children. The groups may come together around a common interest or need or may simply be several children the caregiver thinks would work well together. In a small-group setting, the adult can give children more focused attention, be more responsive to individuals, and provide support and challenges tailored to their individual levels. He can notice what every child is able to do and where each has difficulty. Giving children the opportunity to engage with peers and solve problems collaboratively is yet another major plus of small-group time.

Environments for play. Play space for young infants is relatively small, but expands as infants become mobile. Spaces need to be safe, with play objects children can reach, pick up, handle, and explore. For toddlers, part of the classroom is typically divided into learning centers, or interest areas that offer children a range of options for engagement. Commonly found centers include dramatic play, book corner, manipulatives, discovery/science, and perhaps art. Multipurpose areas are often used for activities such as music, movement,

Basics of Developmentally Appropriate Practice

or cooking. Climbing structures, slides, and even wheel toys are often found indoors as well as outdoors as toddlers have a great need to move their bodies most of the time. The play that takes place in interest areas such as blocks and dramatic play is vital to children's learning and development (see **What Good Is Play?** on page 23). For each area, the teacher carefully selects materials and activities to provide experiences that support educational goals. She also makes a point of observing what children are doing in each area, in order to guide later planning.

Creating environments that encourage relationships is very important in developmentally appropriate practice. This is especially true for infants, but also important for toddlers. The environment needs to include areas for adults (both caregivers and family members) to sit comfortably and chat, spaces for cuddling, and spaces where toddlers can be alone or together. The teacher is on the floor with the children, responding to what they initiate. She thinks about her interactions and, when appropriate, engages the children in conversation. She gives information or feedback, and sometimes models things children might do or say, like saying "Is it time to cook dinner?" while looking in the play kitchen's refrigerator or stirring something on the stove.

Daily routines. As Gopnik states, "Caregivers implicitly and unconsciously teach babies at the same time that they care for them" (2009, 245). It's important to recognize that caregiving routines, those essential activities of daily living, aren't just about meeting basic bodily needs. When caregiving is done hastily, impersonally, or unpredictably, opportunities are lost. Much valuable learning can occur throughout the day in routines such as arrival, departure, room cleanup, diaper changing, dressing, grooming, hand washing, eating, resting, and transitions.

For example, adult and child might sing a song while washing their hands that plays with and highlights the phonological features of language, such as rhyme. This can be thought of as a developmentally appropriate early literacy activity for infants and toddlers. At snack time they might help set out one plate for each place setting, which involves them in exploring one-to-one correspondence that is a foundation for understanding mathematics.

What happens on the diapering table is very important: the caregiver focuses one-on-one on the child and involves her in the process. Rather than a chore to be done quickly, diapering time is an opportunity to build relationships. Creating a feeling of partnership during these times shows respect for children and helps them see themselves as active participants rather than passive recipients, resulting in what can be a lasting spirit of cooperation. Ideally, diapering should be done consistently by the person the infant or toddler knows best, preferably the primary caregiver. The close, personal attention that occurs in a series of intimate interactions solidifies the relationship and fosters trust—an important prerequisite for learning. For infants, eating is another experience that should add to their feelings of security. Bottle-fed infants should be held, and spoon-feeding should take into consideration each infant's skills, needs, likes, and dislikes.

In infant-toddler programs, the caregiving routines of diapering and toileting, sleeping, eating, and transitions truly is the curriculum.

Responsive caregiving is the path to relationships and an important prerequisite for learning. Being responsive means that after the caregiver sets out to do something with a child, she pays attention to how the child responds and then acts accordingly. Responsive caregiving also means that the caregiver allows the child to initiate some actions, rather than always taking the lead herself. To be sensitive to each child, the caregiver must learn to read each child's cues. To engage families in discussion regarding their ideas, goals, and procedures so you can mirror what families do at home is important.

Skills practiced and applied during daily routines are often practical and functional, and thus especially meaningful for children. Meal times and other routines are times when children engage with one another, and caregivers and teachers have excellent opportunities to engage children in more extended conversation.

"Routine" means the usual pattern of activity; something repetitive. That may sound boring to an adult, but it's far from boring for infants and toddlers. It's very important. Hammond emphasizes the importance of routine:

> Routine provides a framework so that each day need not be a new invention, but is an opportunity to fine tune one's orientation to the world. It takes on the spirit of beloved ritual which nurtures relationships as much as bodies. (2009, 43)

3. Plan Appropriate Curriculum

Imagine a river as a metaphor for infant-toddler development—in some places a river meanders, and in others it runs straight and swift. When we develop curriculum for very young children, it can help to keep the idea of the river in mind. Caregivers and teachers don't just watch the river flow. In some ways, the teacher acts like a riverkeeper, shoring up the banks, clearing debris, and following its diversions, but always helping the water to move along its course. Teachers and caregivers carefully observe children, and, most importantly, create relationships and build trust through thoughtful and personal interactions. Trust is what keeps the child's development moving along its course; trust facilitates the flow of the current. Establishing trust is always a dynamic process; infants and toddlers learn to trust their caregivers and teachers, which in turn engenders trust in themselves.

Attuned adults honor young children's learning and developmental process, which is bound to meander sometimes. Learning and development never moves in a straight line. Like a river, it may even slip into side streams. Teachers must resist the temptation to push ahead to achieve goals and objectives, in order to appreciate where the current actually leads.

Curriculum for infants is different from curriculum for toddlers. As Lally states, "Babies come into care with their own learning agenda—their own

curriculum. Armed with an inborn motivation to learn and explore, they are on a constant quest for knowledge, learning from what they see, hear, feel, taste, and touch" (2009, 47). The caregiver learns what the infant needs and is interested in, and only then identifies and plans for the next steps.

A good deal of the caregiver's facilitation of the curriculum happens during caregiving routines such as diapering, feeding, washing, and grooming. Once basic needs are taken care of in intimate and caring interactions, the infant can manage the remainder of the curriculum more or less on his own. When caregivers meet infants' basic needs for food, sleep, and cleanliness in ways that foster close relationships, then satisfied infants are ready for free play.

During free play, the caregiver's role is to be available and responsive, adding language to situations when appropriate. (Of course, a part of the teacher and caregiver's job is also to create a safe environment with appropriate play objects and other babies.) Supporting problem solving is also an important role, as children can learn from the earliest months that they are capable problem solvers. The curriculum during free play focuses on the infant's learning through exploration. However, this does not mean that the adult role is passive—caregivers and teachers take an active approach when they do things such as play peekaboo, sing songs, model how to turn pages in a book, or help infants to explore a toy. The difference is that the adult's active response is within the context of, and in reaction to, the infant's exploration. Moving freely and using their senses in exploration is how infants learn. That's why Piaget called the first two years the "sensorimotor period" (1952).

Most of the interactions adults have with infants from moment to moment are responsive rather than planned out ahead of time. Yet, infant teachers do much that is intentional based on their thinking about where each baby is in his or her development and where they are as a group. The curriculum for infants may be unfixed, but most teachers and caregivers need specialized training to become part of an overall plan, philosophy, or approach. Some of these plans are already drawn out, but others can be invented by the staff and parents through collaboration. Readers can find a variety of useful sources for thinking about infant curriculum in the **References** and **Resources** sections of this book (e.g., Gonzalez-Mena & Stonehouse 2008; Petersen & Wittmar 2009).

For toddlers, it is vital for every program to have a curriculum or a plan for learning in mind or in written form, and to actually use it to guide planning. The curriculum guides teachers in observing, developing, and carrying out learning experiences that are consistent with the program's goals for children and connect within an organized framework.

Like an infant, the individual toddler is still the basis for the curriculum—and many of the same principles used for infants apply to toddlers. For example, individual interests should influence the setup of the environment and plans for learning. Diapering continues to be a one-on-one experience, and the timing of toilet learning may also be individual (although toddlers can also be influenced by what others in the group are learning).

> A good toddler teacher selects the best strategy and provides just the right amount of support for that child and that situation.

Toddlers are more able to see themselves as part of a group, so group interests begin to influence teachers' plans. Caregiving times are an important part of the curriculum as toddlers learn both as individuals and group members. Learning to eat in groups is another important part of the curriculum. By toddlerhood, settling down and going to sleep may well be a group activity.

One critical aspect of the curriculum, problem solving, is just as important for toddlers as it is for infants. When teachers think of supporting the development of problem-solving processes as curriculum, they are less likely to step in with their own solution when they see a child having a difficulty. Say a toy isn't working the way a toddler wants it to. It's tempting to rescue that child, especially if she is frustrated. Instead of showing the child how the toy works, use this situation as a teaching strategy and let the child work on the problem. If the child is about to give up, step in and offer a small amount of help. It takes skill and practice to decide when and how to offer tiny hints, but the child's inner feeling of satisfaction is immense when she makes something happen through her own efforts.

Of course, planned activities are also part of the curriculum, but it's important to think of the kinds of activities that encourage exploration rather than those that have just one way to do them or have a predetermined outcome. Toddlers are still learning how the world works, and their exploratory urges are necessarily strong.

Key learning outcomes for children

Curriculum development and planning begin with the question, What kinds of experiences in this program will promote development and learning to each child's full potential? Teachers must also ask, What goals or outcomes do we want the children to achieve during the time that we are working with them? The "we" in this case is greater than just the teacher, and should always include the child's family. The selection of goals and outcomes is also often influenced by other parties such as program administrators and funding agents, as well as by state or national standards.

Good programs have always recognized that children's early physical, social, emotional, and cognitive development affects their future success and well-being, and programs have actively sought (in collaboration with families) to promote development and learning in all these areas. Over the years the research base has grown, and now we are able to define more specifically which outcomes enable children to succeed in school and beyond.

As vital as ever is supporting children's curiosity, self-regulation, social competence, and sense of their own capacity to learn and achieve. Developing social and emotional skills—such as the ability to make friends or to regulate one's feelings and reactions—has proven important to how children fare later on in school and in their personal relationships. Among the areas where we need to place greater emphasis than in the past, however, are vocabulary and language proficiency, early literacy foundations (e.g., playing with sounds, experience with books, awareness of print and its uses), and key beginning mathematics and science ideas.

In recent years professional organizations, states, and other entities have been placing greater emphasis on defining and evaluating key learning out-comes for school-age children. This trend has now reached early childhood programs, with most states as well as Head Start programs articulating specific learning outcomes for children to achieve by the end of preschool. Some learn-ing outcomes focus on infants and toddlers specifically.

For example, WestEd (an educational research, development, and service agency that offers a national training program for infant-toddler caregivers) defines a number of research-based outcomes at 8 months, 18 months, and

36 months (California Dept. of Education & WestEd Center for Child and Family Studies 2009). The following are just a few examples of key learning outcomes for children birth to age 3, based on the WestEd findings as well as other research (Galinsky 2010; Tardos 2007):

In intellectual development—

- ◆ At 8 months, children explore different features of objects (e.g., lifting the flaps of cloth books to see the images underneath).
- ◆ At 18 months, children engage in symbolic play (e.g., pretending to drink from an empty cup).
- ◆ At 36 months, children pay attention to more than one thing at a time (e.g., they can experiment intently with playdough while simultaneously describing what they are doing).

In emotional development—

- ◆ At 8 months, children express their feelings and needs through crying and other behavior, facial expressions, and body language (e.g., indicating the discomfort of a full diaper by crying).
- ◆ At 18 months, children express their feelings and needs using words, sounds, body language, gestures, and crying (e.g., shaking head vehemently while saying No! when refusing to do something).
- ◆ At 36 months, children often express their feelings using words only or words plus actions (e.g., asking "I have milk?" while tugging at the refrigerator door.

In social-emotional development—

- ◆ At 8 months, children imitate simple actions and expressions (e.g., waving back when someone waves at them).
- ◆ At 18 months, children imitate actions with more than one step (e.g., pretending to wash dishes in the dramatic play area and then putting them away).
- ◆ At 36 months, children imitate many actions observed in the past (e.g., hosting a pretend birthday party in the sandbox).

Making curriculum effective

As part of its standards for accreditation of early childhood programs nation-wide, NAEYC (2007) has identified as essential the curriculum areas listed below. All these areas are important for children's learning and well-being. With minor differences here and there, this list is representative of the curriculum areas defined as important by many professional groups and states:

◆ Social-emotional development

◆ Language development

◆ Literacy development

◆ Mathematics

◆ Technology, scientific inquiry and knowledge

◆ Understanding ourselves and our communities

◆ Creative expression and appreciation for the arts

◆ Physical development and skills

A good curriculum for infants and toddlers addresses all these areas, though in some cases it is laying early foundations rather than targeting the domain more directly. Obviously social-emotional, physical, and language development are critical curriculum areas. Literacy is tied to language development and early experiences with print. Understanding ourselves and where we belong is vital in the earliest years. Creative expression is a constant, but developing appreciation for the arts is not so obvious in the first three years of life. Likewise, literacy, mathematics, and science and technology have roots in the first three years but don't look the same as in programs for older children.

A good curriculum is much more than a collection of activities; it includes everything that happens in a program. It is based on keeping key outcomes in mind, and it should provide teachers and caregivers with a useful framework for interacting with children, embedding language into those interactions, and encouraging children's problem solving. An important aspect of the infant-toddler curriculum is setting up the environment to promote development and support learning experiences that accomplish the outcomes.

However a program arrives at its curriculum, the curriculum should be both effective and comprehensive—that is, addressing all areas of children's development and learning. Published, commercially available curriculum products, if they are consistent with the recommendations of the profession (see, e.g., NAEYC & NAECS/SDE 2003) and with the program's goals, may be worth considering for use. Or, if program staff themselves have the interest, expertise, and resources to develop a curriculum, the program may decide to take that route.

In addition to making sure the curriculum is comprehensive and developmentally appropriate, teachers should do the following:

Use the curriculum framework when planning in order to give coherence to the program experiences.

A developmentally appropriate curriculum for children under 3 places a great deal of emphasis on relationships and responsiveness to children as individuals. Sensitivity to each child's needs and interests is of the highest priority. Ratios and group size make a difference in such a curriculum. At the same time, the curriculum and daily experiences must be well thought out. As valuable as it is to use spontaneous opportunities in teaching, there must be an overall plan

---

Adapt, articulate, advocate

What if you're not in a position to make the decision about what curriculum will be adopted for the program? As a teacher or caregiver, this choice may not be in your hands. But even if this is the case, you are likely to have a role in selecting from choices the curriculum offers and adapting its learning experiences. When you are able to articulate clearly how your adaptations will contribute to the curriculum's goals, you are more likely to be given the flexibility to make those changes.

Another possibility is that you are working in a program that either doesn't have a written curriculum or has one in name only—a curriculum book or kit, perhaps, gathering dust on the shelf rather than serving as the mainspring for planning. When teachers and caregivers encounter this situation, it's vital they be proactive in designing or choosing a clear curriculum plan for their group and making sure it gets used.

---

in which close attention is paid to matching curriculum to children's individual skill and developmental levels. We must be familiar with the key experiences and skills in each domain (the **Resources** section lists sources of guidance for each domain). Then, we must do careful planning and follow-through, carefully shaping and adapting the experiences we provide to enable each child to acquire these concepts and skills according to their individual level of development.

Consider the developmental paths that children follow in determining the sequence and pace of learning experiences.

Teachers continually observe and consider environmental arrangements, materials, and activities with an eye to supporting children's development and learning in all areas. As we've stressed earlier, infants and toddlers acquire a great deal of knowledge during essential daily activities, such as feeding and eating. We must pay careful attention to how children's development occurs sequentially within the concept of these routines. Among the concepts and skills we want children to acquire, some things logically come first and other things build on them. For example, children need to manipulate objects first in order to gain a basic understanding of their characteristics, only then are they capable of selecting those items in the group that are alike.

We also want to select materials with individual children's interests and developmental progress in mind. Here's an example:

> Lisa notices that Haylee grabs the spoon when she is feeding her. She isn't yet ready to feed herself, but Lisa notes that she wants to try. She gives Haylee a spoon while she continues to feed her, and provides a toy bowl and spoon for Haylee to play with.

Make meaningful connections a priority in curriculum planning.

Connected, integrated curriculum is more effective than curriculum content taught in small, unrelated chunks. We need to remember too that learning something new is easier when it builds on something we already know. Young children in particular learn best when the concepts, vocabulary, and skills they encounter are related to something they know and care about, and when the new learnings are themselves interconnected in meaningful, coherent ways.

Basics of Developmentally Appropriate Practice

There are several common approaches to making children's learning integrated and meaningful. Themes or simple projects such as planting seeds or painting a mural together can help 2- and 3-year-olds see how concepts and skills are related and how these matter. But for infants and young toddlers the connections are mostly in the mind of the adult. The daily routine is what connects things for the youngest children.

As always, whether determining projects or themes or just setting up the play area with appropriate objects, teachers and caregivers can draw on children's own interests and can also introduce them to new things that might appeal to them. Developing and extending children's interests is part of a good curriculum; depth is important, too. Sometimes adults hurry through an activity out of concern that children will lose attention. However, infants and toddlers become more engaged in meaningful learning when the curriculum allows for sustained time with any given experience. Slowing down allows children the opportunity to become thoroughly involved in what interests them—their attention spans are much longer than we imagine! Sustained time allows for meaningful, integrated, and in-depth learning.

4. Assess Children's Development and Learning

Curriculum is the plan for enabling children to reach their full and unique potential; it's also about desired outcomes. Assessment is the process of looking at children's progress toward that potential and those outcomes. In the earliest years, assessment needs to be based on expectations of typical development within a given area. As Petersen and Wittmer state, "Assessment involves observing a child's performance compared to certain skills that usually appear in a predictable order or within a certain age range" (2009, 102).

Thoughtful attention to assessment is essential to developmentally appropriate practice. Assessing children, which includes observing them and closely considering their progress, is key for teachers in their efforts to get to know each child and his or her abilities and needs. Thus, it is a vital part of "meeting learners where they are." On an ongoing basis, a teacher needs to assess each child to determine whether he or she is making progress toward important outcomes and to inform the planning necessary to promote that child's learning and development.

In developmentally appropriate programs, we assess in order to

◆ Monitor children's development and learning

- ◆ Guide our planning and decision making
- ◆ Identify children who might benefit from special services or supports
- ◆ Report and communicate with others (McAfee et al. 2004)

Assessment of young children's learning and progress is vital, but it requires certain understandings. In their early years, children grow and change rapidly. Their development is uneven, full of spurts and plateaus. Therefore, assessment by teachers and caregivers should be ongoing and integrated into the daily routine.

Information about individual children's learning and progress should be gathered from various sources (including parents or other important family

---

Using assessment information effectively

As teachers we don't gather information about children just to let it sit on the shelf. And those observation notes you make on little scraps? Don't leave them stuffed in your pockets. *Use* the information as you plan and teach. Experts (Jablon et al. 2007; McAfee et al. 2004) on how to make good use of assessment information offer suggestions such as these:

Plan on a daily, weekly, and long-term basis in order to provide what children need to learn and thrive.

Some caregivers write out their plans in detail; others do their planning in broader strokes, adding notes relating to specific activities and individual children. Whatever method you choose, you will need to reflect and plan thoughtfully for the group as a whole and for each individual child.

Consider all relevant assessment information as you plan.

Refer to your observation notes on each child, and the information you have gathered from families. You may also use other forms of assessment, such as a specific tool.

Use assessment information to individualize for children.

Observing children during daily routines and noting how they use the environment and what they gravitate toward will help you determine how to adapt the environment, materials, or daily routines to be responsive to individual children's interests, needs, and strengths.

For example, in recording how children use different areas—such as noting who looks at books—you might notice that a particular child, Shawn, is too busy running around the room to engage with a book. You would then give some thought to what might interest Shawn and bring

---

Basics of Developmentally Appropriate Practice

members), at various times, and in different settings or contexts. Norm-referenced assessments of infants and toddlers for that purpose are inappropriate. Also, don't assess toddlers using purely verbal procedures—these tend to underestimate children's knowledge and cognitive skills, especially for dual-language learners (NAEYC 2005).

Families are a primary source of assessment information. Teachers and caregivers can gather information from families by observing parents with their children. Such observations should be done more than just during arrival and departure times, which are often the worst times of the day for parents. Home visits are a wonderful way to get to know families and see infants and toddlers in their familiar surroundings. Of course, intake interviews, parent conferences,

in some books you think would appeal to him. You might read one of these with him, either one-on-one or including another child as well, and offer another if he asks. Over time, continue to entice him to sit with you and look at the books, and observe for a few weeks to see whether his interest in books increases.

Or suppose you are helping children to understand and express how objects are located in relation to each other. For the children who don't yet know *in*, *out*, *next to*, and other basic location words, plan various opportunities through which they can learn these through movement and using their bodies. A simple obstacle course might work, or even an enclosure made from cardboard boxes.

Don't try to go it alone.

Look to professional organizations, such as NAEYC, WestEd's Program for Infant/Toddler Care, and Zero to Three, for guidance on assessment and curriculum, and for information about children's development and learning (see the **Resources** section for some suggestions). Other sources are commercial curriculum guides and the curriculum guidance produced by states or programs.

Consider modifications to routines or the learning environment.

Time, space, materials, learning contexts, and adult roles can all be modified to help meet children's assessed needs. For example, almost anything you do with children can be made simpler or more complex, according to what individual children are ready for.

Make follow-up plans.

Children generally need repeated experiences with an idea or skill to get a solid grasp, but not so often that it becomes old. Follow through to ensure children really master the skill or concept. Give careful thought to where the child or group of children might go next.

and meetings—both formal and causal—can all be times when information flows back and forth between professionals and families.

Gathering assessment evidence from observing in realistic situations is key. Ongoing, regular observations within the natural environment are more likely to reflect what children do on an everyday basis and reveal the full extent of what they are capable of doing and understanding. To round out this picture, observations should occur across different settings, such as indoors, outside, and during interactions with peers, familiar adults, and strangers. Assessments should also occur in activities across all the domains of the curriculum, including essential daily activities.

Keeping written records is essential to keep track of where each child is in all areas of development and detail what they can do. It helps to focus on what children can do rather than on what they can't.

Finally, as we have seen in other areas of teacher decision making, assessing children in developmentally appropriate ways requires attention to what is

◆ Age-appropriate—anticipating the characteristics of children within an age range that are likely to influence the validity of our assessment methods

◆ Individually appropriate—which includes choosing and adapting our means of assessment to get the best information about a particular child

◆ Culturally appropriate—for example, considering what will make sense to the child, given her linguistic and cultural background, as well as interpreting her behaviors in light of the social and cultural contexts in which she lives (e.g., that if a dual-language learner struggles to respond to questions asked in English, it doesn't mean she is deficient in either language or intellect)

5. Develop Reciprocal Relationships with Families

For infants and toddlers, this aspect of developmentally appropriate practice is the most crucial. Making developmentally appropriate decisions for the infants and toddlers in a group means knowing them as individuals. And the younger the children, the more a teacher needs to acquire much of this knowledge through relationships with their families. Asking families about their children is an extremely valuable strategy, but that's not all. It also conveys to parents that teachers value their knowledge and insights.

A good teacher never displays a condescending attitude—that *she's* the one with all the information and best equipped to make all the decisions and that parents are basically uninformed folks badly needing her wisdom to make good choices for their children. Of course, for parents of a new baby who is the first in the family, the caregiver may have information about infant care that parents don't. But don't assume that. The parents may have knowledge from helping raise younger siblings, or from a variety of other sources. Perhaps they have family elders as resources, with experience in infant care specific to a particular culture.

> Reciprocal relationships require mutual respect, cooperation, shared responsibility, and negotiation of differences toward shared goals.

No matter how much the caregiver knows, parents are the most important people in their children's lives. They know their child well, and their preferences and choices matter. The relationship we want to create is a two-way street, with communication and respect in both directions—that is, a reciprocal relationship.

Besides drawing on families' in-depth knowledge of their children as individuals, effective teachers will also learn from families about their home and community environment, including its cultural dimensions. This knowledge is critical in making program decisions that are appropriate for children, as well as in fostering positive relationships with the parents themselves.

The other side of the reciprocal relationship is this: Early childhood teachers have a lot to share with families. We have valuable knowledge and experience with children in general. And we can give parents the particulars about what their own child said and did that day, what he is exploring, interested in, curious about, and achieving in the program. Family members greatly value this information and love to hear about these moments in their young child's life. In addition, when they learn about the child's life in the program, they are better able to build on these experiences at home.

Teacher-parent communication is important, too, in achieving a degree of consistency in the ways that the significant adults in the child's life guide and relate to that child. There isn't likely to be much consistency without communication. Still another plus is that children feel more secure when they see that the adults who care about them—their parents and teachers, in this case—are themselves in a positive relationship and share trust and respect.

When it comes to making decisions about a child, sharing that decision making with families is important. Making "common cause" around a goal is a good starting point for a partnership with a family. Here is an example of parents and caregivers seeing things differently. Notice what this caregiver does about it.

> Sophia is crawling and gets around very well. Her mother takes her caregiver, Tory, aside one day and asks why they don't have walkers in the center. She thinks that walkers would help Sophia learn to walk faster. Tory explains about the danger of walkers and offers an article with some research on the subject. She also asks the mother to come in early one day and join her in observing her daughter. The two watch how Sophia is so very interested in everything within reach and how she chooses certain objects to

manipulate and thoroughly explore. Then they watch a child who is new at walking—he moves around the room with great concentration on staying upright, and pays no attention to the toys on the floor. The mother notices the difference. Tory asks for her observations, and Sophia's mother says, "I guess what she's into right now is what is convenient to her. Walking is a whole different thing and it's hard to walk while playing with the toys. I think you're trying to show me that what she's doing right now is just what she needs to be doing. When she starts walking she'll have different skills and interests for awhile." Tory grins and nods her head. "Yes!" she says enthusiastically.

The box **Creating Two-Way Relationships with Families** summarizes some general guidelines in making such relationships a reality.

Now the star is complete, each point connected to every other point. Creating a community of learners, teaching, curriculum, assessment, and developing relationships with families—all are integral parts of the whole that is early childhood practice.

If you are reading this book, it's very likely that you have a strong desire to contribute to children's lives. To make sure your efforts succeed, you will need to take seriously all five aspects of practice and continually deepen and update your knowledge within each of them. Then the children you teach will learn and thrive.

FAQs

Questions about Developmentally Appropriate Practice

As we talk with caregivers, teachers, administrators, parents, and policymakers about developmentally appropriate practice, we get asked all sorts of questions. This section covers the most common ones—with the recognition that our responses are always evolving over time. They change as the research base expands but also as a result of the conversations we have with others. We offer these answers, then, not as the "last word" on what are hard questions, but rather to foster further conversations among all early childhood educators.

How can I recognize a developmentally appropriate infant-toddler program?

You can tell if an infant-toddler program is developmentally appropriate in several ways. Watch the interactions between adults and children—they should be warm and caring; in fact, the whole atmosphere should be hospitable and convey a sense of "You are welcome here." Look for a good adult-to-child ratio. Observe how the teachers read each child's cues in order to meet their needs. Watch how they treat the children during those essential activities of daily living such as diapering. Are they fully focused on the child and creating a warm, caring, and intimate experience, or are diaperings rushed through as a tedious chore? Can you see evidence of a primary caregiver system, where each child connects not only with a team of teachers but also with one special teacher? Check out the environment, does it give messages to the children and families that say, "You belong here—no matter culture, background, or where you are from"? Is the environment set up in such a way that the children want to engage in exploring it? Do you see learning going on? Is the environment reflective of the ages and stages of the children in it? Does the program accommodate children with special needs in ways that give them the most freedom to explore, develop, and learn?

Do proponents of DAP think that there is only one right way to work with infants and toddlers?

Actually, developmentally appropriate practice means just the opposite. Individual children vary greatly in their development, prior experience, abilities, preferences, and interests, and there is no formula that works for them all. Moreover, to teach any child effectively, teachers and caregivers must use a variety of approaches and strategies and make intentional choices about what to use in a particular situation. As we describe in the chapter **Teach to Enhance Development and Learning,** good infant-toddler teachers acknowledge, support, encourage, and create challenges that extend children's learning and development. Children often pick up and imitate the behavior of those around them, and teachers and caregivers are always modeling behavior, whether consciously or not. That's very indirect teaching, but it's powerful. Of course, teachers of infants and toddlers will also teach directly by giving specific information, but children should first be encouraged to see if they can figure things out themselves.

Is "Developmentally Appropriate Practice" a curriculum?

No, DAP is not a curriculum. It is a set of guidelines that can be used to help educators make decisions about curriculum as well as teaching strategies for supporting and promoting development and learning. *Curriculum* can be defined in many ways, but the most basic definition is usually that curriculum is the *what*—that is, the content and the plans for experiences that support development and learning. Planning curriculum that is appropriate for children is certainly one aspect of DAP, but there is not a particular curriculum that is designated as "developmentally appropriate practice."

There are a variety of early childhood curriculum approaches that are based on the underlying principles of child development and learning that undergird the NAEYC guidelines for developmentally appropriate practice. There are also many commercially developed curriculum products that reflect diverse theoretical perspectives on learning and development and provide more or less structure and support for the teacher. Principles of developmentally appropriate practice should always be applied in developing, selecting, and implementing a curriculum.

At the same time, whatever the curriculum model, it can only be truly effective and developmentally appropriate if teachers understand how children generally learn and develop, and if they adapt their teaching materials, experiences, and strategies to meet those children's individual needs. Curriculum matters, but it does not take the place of a good teacher.

I have become the director of a program with several infant-toddler classrooms in which the teachers are warm, loving people but they could do more to facilitate learning and support development in the children. What can I do to improve the quality in these classrooms without losing these caregivers?

Observe individual teachers, and note how each interacts with individual children. Consider this information to help you decide how to work with the individuals and with the group. When observing, give feedback to the teachers, describing what you see and putting special emphasis on the positive behaviors you notice. Encourage the teachers to pay attention to each child in order to read cues about what the child needs and also what interests him or her. Help the teachers discover the values of being responsive to what the child initiates. Model this responsive behavior yourself. Help them understand that facilitating learning involves supporting development and keying into the child's interests rather than pushing them forward. The point is to help each child, starting in infancy, feel good about him or herself as a learner. When learning is self-motivated early in life, it doesn't depend on praise or other reward systems. Moving forward is itself a reward for the child.

Help the teachers observe a child and ask them to talk about what this child can do. Help them describe in detail just how the child does what he is able to do. (Video can be helpful here.) Discuss where they see the child's growing edge. Ask them how the child can be encouraged to do what he can already do even better rather than pushing for the next steps this child will take. Teach them to be good observers and help them see how what the child is doing now relates to those next steps.

Most importantly, help the teachers understand the connection between adult-child relationships and learning. The more secure the child feels in the relationship, the more able he is to learn.

Those are short answers to a question that can involve years of learning, but the advice here is a good start.

Are developmentally appropriate programs unstructured?

The idea that there is very little or no structure in a DAP classroom is a misconception. Again, in reality the opposite is true. To be developmentally appropriate, a program must be thoughtfully structured to build on and advance children's competence. For this reason, a developmentally appropriate program is well organized in its routines and physical environment and uses a planned curriculum to guide teachers as they support children in their learning and development. The structure of a developmentally appropriate program is not rigid, however. Instead it permits adaptation for individual variation and is flexible, so as to accommodate children's interests and progress.

In the developmentally appropriate program, there is a predictable but not rigid schedule to the day, with clear limits so children learn what is acceptable behavior and what is not. Children are in an environment where they have opportunities to move freely, and within the course of the day are presented with appropriate objects, equipment, and experiences. Exercise occurs outdoors and in, and the environment is set up to foster children's climbing, balancing, and other physical skills. For infants and toddlers, physical skills are closely tied to intellectual development, and also contribute to social-emotional goals. The teacher is intentional in using the environment and everything in it to enable children to acquire important knowledge and skills.

Someone told me that in DAP classrooms, all children do is play. Is that true?

Research shows that self-initiated, teacher-supported play benefits children in many ways. When infants and toddlers play, they engage in many important tasks, such as developing and practicing newly acquired skills and regulating emotions and behaviors. As they grow out of infancy, play includes making friends, using language creatively, eventually taking turns, and learning to respond appropriately to the demands of the situation. This is why infants and toddlers need to play for a large part of the day, when they aren't otherwise involved in essential activities such as eating and diaper changing.

Play is an important part of a developmentally appropriate program. At first, young infants' play is exploratory and manipulative as they grasp, hold, mouth, and drop various play objects. Infants in groups might also explore each other while an ever watchful caregiver teaches them to be gentle. For toddlers, effective teachers often take action to enhance and support children's play and the learning that goes on in the play context. They may engage in one-on-one conversations with children and encourage pretend play with themes, roles, guidance, and props—all of which research shows is related to both language and literacy development. (For more on this, see the box **What Good Is Play?** on page 23.)

But play is not the only thing that children do in developmentally appropriate programs. They also participate in enriching routines, which become important learning experiences as they engage with teachers and peers, acquire self-help skills, and learn how to help others. Toddlers may also work in small groups, listen to stories, and perhaps occasionally meet in a larger group. An important part of learning and development involves problem solving, which may happen during play or other times. Allowing infants and toddlers to solve their own problems rather than rescuing them may not fit all parents' ideas of good practice, but it is an important way for children to learn.

The flip side of the play question also arises: In light of current demands for improving learning outcomes and narrowing the achievement gap, is play still a major component of DAP?

Yes, it certainly is. The 2009 position statement says more about play than any previous statement has done (NAEYC 2009). In fact, as the relevant knowledge base has grown, there is more to say about play—its enormous value, its endangered status in today's media-intensive world, and what teachers can do to enable all children to reach the higher levels of play that are most conducive for promoting self-regulation and other aspects of development and learning.

I like to teach in my own style. Would DAP stifle my individuality as a teacher?

Teachers are individuals, just as children are. We each have our own interests, abilities, preferences, social and cultural contexts, and unique experiences that make us who we are. Developmentally appropriate practice calls for the teacher to create a caring community of learners, an important member of which is the teacher. Teachers should bring their unique selves, including their talents and interests, into the program. If a teacher is artistic, musical, literary, athletic, or whatever, she should be able to draw on her own style in her teaching, because it probably reflects her strengths (see, e.g., Alati 2005, in **Resources**).

The important thing to remember is not every child will share the teacher's preferred style. To be effective, you must understand how the *children* learn and develop, and use a variety of strategies to meet those children's individual needs as well as the needs of the group.

I think DAP makes sense, but the families I serve have different ideas about how their children should be cared for and taught. What should I do?

Begin by dropping the jargon when you communicate with families. Don't use the terms "DAP" or even "developmentally appropriate practice." Instead, have a conversation with families about your ideas, plans, and goals for the program, as well as what they want and expect.

Negotiating differences begins with you clearly understanding your own preferences and where they come from. This might take your doing some serious thinking and reflecting first. Then communicate about your point of view and listen, truly *listen,* to the family's concerns. When you and the family articulate your respective goals, it is likely that you can find common ground. Be open to learning from family members and willing to expand your view of effective, developmentally appropriate practice based on what you learn. In a successful negotiation, families also learn and change. If you just give in to parents' demands, you will lose self-respect and probably effectiveness; if parents just give in to your position, they lose their power in their relationship with you and in their children's lives. In either case, children ultimately lose. The goal is a win-win outcome in which teacher and family learn from each other and come up with a solution that works for both.

I want my child to be ready to succeed in school. Doesn't he need more than DAP in his program?

Developmentally appropriate programs richly contribute to children's learning and development. One of the well-documented research findings about high-quality, developmentally appropriate early childhood programs is that they do prepare children for later success in school, especially children living in poverty (Bowman et al. 2000; Schweinhart & Weikart 1997; U.S. Dept. of Health and Human Services 2006). A good program helps children acquire the kind of foundation they need for later school learning, gaining competencies in three key areas: mind, feelings, and body. This means that they gain thinking skills (e.g., using language effectively), learn to recognize and experience their emotions (e.g., positively using the energy that accompanies strong feelings), and learn to use their bodies effectively (e.g., gaining strength and balance). They also learn to get along with others and care about them.

In the earliest years, it's important to recognize the interconnectedness of the foundational learning areas important to later school learning—they always go together! So, if children are not making learning and developmental progress toward the important outcomes of those foundational areas, then the program is not developmentally appropriate.

I teach children with disabilities. Is there a conflict between DAP and the methods used in special education?

Children with disabilities are children first. They share most of the same developmental and learning needs and have many of the same strengths as their typically developing peers. The DAP principles of meeting children where they are and creating challenging and achievable goals are just as important for children with disabilities. Further, we know from decades of research in early childhood special education that children with disabilities benefit most from being served in inclusive settings, that is, places where they would be found if they did not have a disability (Odom et al. 2002; Sandall et al. 2000).

Teachers and caregivers of infants and toddlers with identified disabilities should be part of a team that includes specialists and families and that develops and implements an Individualized Family Service Plan (IFSP) for the child. The plan, along with participation in the inclusive setting, should ensure that the child makes desired progress toward the shared goals of the family and the program.

My program serves children from a variety of cultures, and I'm wondering whether DAP is the best thing for them. Is DAP for all children or just for some children?

The principles of developmentally appropriate practice call for teachers to pay attention to the social and cultural contexts in which the children live and take these into account in shaping the environment for development and learning.

Whatever children's prior experiences or cultural expectations are, caregivers and teachers help them to make sense of new experiences. At times, this situation may require explicit teaching of limits or skills that the child has not previously encountered. Or it will require the teacher to recognize that children can acquire the same skills and ideas through different experiences and routines. For example, in some cultures, babies are spoon-fed longer than others; teachers can recognize that feeding a baby the same way her mother does will someday lead to self-feeding, though the timing may be different from what's expected by the other families in the program. Most important, the classroom must be a welcoming environment that demonstrates respect and support for all families and their children's contexts.

I am sometimes daunted by the circumstances of children growing up in poverty. Will DAP enable them to catch up and be ready for school?

This is a good question, and the answer is "yes, but . . ." Closing the performance gap between children of low-income families and middle-class families is a formidable task, and it needs to be tackled early in children's lives. Early interventions, which can even start prenatally, are crucial in moving children from low-income families closer to children from middle-income families in language development and other areas (Tough 2009; U.S. Dept. of Health and Human Services 2006). Clearly, programs serving children of low-income families need to give special attention to language development if children are to perform at the same level as their middle-class peers.

Without intervention, differences in children's early environments can be staggering. For example, a child in a professional family on average hears 11 million words a year, while a child in a family of low income hears just 3 million (Hart & Risley 1995). In the earliest years, adult responses to infants' vocalizations are crucial in building early oral language skills. Babbling is the precursor to language, and adults can increase babbling by responding to it. This is important to recognize because adults who worry about vocabulary deficits tend to talk nonstop with infants, flooding them with language. However, a study of infants and mothers found that "how often a mother initiated a conversation with her child was not predictive of the language outcomes—what mattered was, if the infant initiated, whether the mom responded" (Bronson & Merryman 2009, 208). By toddlerhood, the children of high-responding mothers were six months ahead in language development compared with those of mothers who weren't so responsive. This is important information for parents and caregivers. As Magda Gerber stressed, being responsive to what the infant initiates is very important, and the research backs that up.

Caregivers working with dual-language learners have the additional challenge of ensuring that those children continue to maintain and develop their home language. Many adults worry that learning two languages will confuse and delay language development in infants and toddlers. However, research indicates this is not true—in fact, it is very important to give special attention to supporting home language learning in infant-toddler programs (Stechuk et al. 2006). Further, as Tabors states, "What research has shown is that the bilingual children who do best in school are those who have had a strong grounding in their home language" (2008, 131).

The principles and guidelines of developmentally appropriate practice certainly should underlie all our efforts to serve all these children and their families well. If we truly meet the learners where they are and help them to reach challenging and achievable goals, as DAP requires, we will promote their learning and development to their great long-term benefit. But, as dramatically shown by evidence such as that of Hart and Risley, some children have ground to make up. So teachers and caregivers need to be knowledgeable about the learning needs of the children they teach and the teaching strategies with proven success in helping such children reach higher levels of achievement. The **Resources** list provided at the end of this book includes a number of publications (e.g., Kovach & Ros-Voseles 2008; Lally & Mangione 2006) that provide good information to help all children, including the educational and developmental needs of children growing up in poverty and the approaches that seem to be most promising in addressing these.

A key fact that should also be noted is that children and families living with the many stresses of poverty typically need access to comprehensive services including health, nutrition, mental health, and social services. Early Head Start provides these, and there are other programs funded in various ways that also provide comprehensive services to families expecting a baby or who have infants and toddlers. There are not enough of them, but such programs do make a difference. Thus, advocating for these services is important for all those concerned about children's well-being.

I've heard DAP is about not hurrying children, about giving them the gift of time. Is that right?

The expression "gift of time" comes from a valid concern of not expecting too much of children too soon. Giving a child time can be both a benefit and a disservice. Let us explain.

How can time be a benefit? Infants and toddlers each have their own individual developmental timetable. If you push them to reach milestones before they are ready, they may well skip over preliminary skills—the foundations needed for that milestone. For example, you can't really teach a baby to walk. If you try, the results are an unstable walker who needs your help longer than he would otherwise. When the child can get up on his own two feet and balance by himself, he has learned just what his body can do, and progresses from there.

However, allowing for extra time can also do a child a real disservice. Why? It isn't just time that promotes development, it is also what happens while the time passes—the experiences a child has with objects and people. A baby who grows up in a deprived situation, with little opportunity to form positive attachments and explore and learn about the environment and herself, needs more than just time. And infants and toddlers who experience violence— either directly or as witnesses—especially need intervention. A DAP program geared to understanding the individual needs of infants and toddlers can make the kind of difference that just giving a child time can't do.

So DAP does not mean simply waiting until children are "ready." It means setting developmentally appropriate expectations and understanding that, although there are some biological limitations, children's learning experiences will drive their development. For example, 2-year-olds lack the fine motor skills needed to manipulate a pencil and form letters, but digging, playing with clay, and other fine motor activities build up the necessary muscles, while opportunities to scribble and draw help them get ready to write. Maturation is needed, but so is experience.

Where can I get more information about DAP?

This book is an introduction to the basics of DAP. A more detailed description of the principles and concepts is NAEYC's *Developmentally Appropriate Practice in Early Childhood Programs Serving Children from Birth through Age 8* (Copple & Bredekamp 2009). Also, a list of many useful resources for understanding and using developmentally appropriate practice appears in the **Resources** section at the end of this book.

A Changing Picture: Children at 0–9 Months, 8–18 Months, and 16–36 Months

The following charts give a general picture of what children are like in their infant-toddler years—from birth to age 3—and how adults can promote their learning and development.

For each age group we have divided the common characteristics and behaviors into four categories of development (physical, intellectual, social, emotional). But in doing so, we do not mean to imply that the different areas don't overlap, because certainly they do. Likewise, there is considerable overlap between the age groups. Some children will exhibit certain characteristics and behaviors at earlier ages than their peers; others will take longer to acquire a given set of skills and concepts.

In other words, generalizations are only that. It is through close observation and interaction with the individual children in their classrooms that skilled teachers and caregivers assess where children are and so know how to best guide them.

Children ages 0–9 months

What children are like	How adults can help
Physical development	
Newborn babies have limited large muscle movements, which are largely reflexive. From birth through 3 months, infants gradually gain voluntary control over their heads, arms, and legs. From 6 to 9 months, infants gain control over head movements and gain some mobility by rolling from front to back, sitting up, and making progress toward crawling. At 9 months, babies may cruise upright around the room by holding onto furniture; some may be able to stand alone.	Provide safe spaces for babies to explore, such as a mats, rugs, or blankets, and avoid restraining infants in restrictive devices. Place infants on their backs to sleep and to observe their environment and move their limbs; they will also benefit from "tummy time" each day to strengthen their developing head and neck muscles. As infants grow and gain mobility, create challenges by adding pillows, low furniture, and other safe materials to make different levels to climb and pull up on. Playpens should be large enough for adult caregivers to join children.
Infants' small muscle movements are also almost completely reflexive after birth. A newborn will tightly ball his fist to grasp an object, but after three months babies overcome this reflex. They can selectively reach for—and miss—objects placed near them. An infant's eyesight also becomes more coordinated in the first few weeks. By 6 months, babies begin to rake objects toward them using their entire hands, and from 6 to 9 months infants gain control in grasping, manipulating, and exploring objects (often by mouthing). By 9 months babies can use their thumbs and forefingers in a pincer grip to pick up even very small objects.	Gradually increase the number and variety of playthings provided to young infants. Toys like bright cotton scarves, rattles, and balls will motivate babies to grasp and manipulate them with their hands, fingers, and other body parts. By 9 months, offer a cup and spoon as well as toys such as dolls and nesting blocks.

What children are like	How adults can help
Intellectual development	
A newborn baby's reflexes are the beginning of her sensory skills; these in turn are the bases for her developing intellect. During the first nine months, infants' abilities to focus, pay attention, and respond to stimuli gradually increase along with their physical ability to gain control over their body. At 3 months they show signs of remembering, and by 6 months can recognize familiar objects. By 9 months, an infant remembers games and toys from previous days, anticipates a person's return, and can concentrate for periods of time without interruption.	Babies learn rapidly from birth on, primarily from observing and interacting with their primary caregivers. Infants love to look at faces; adults should get close and let children gaze at them during play and caretaking. Give babies the freedom to move about and explore. Place infants with limited mobility on their backs on a safe firm mat so they can move their arms and legs and look around; as babies learn to roll over, crawl, and pull to standing provide them with more space and appropriate low furniture. Provide consistent routines, talk to babies about their actions and activities, and let them interact with other babies.
Babies gradually learn about cause and effect. At 3 months, children will look for the source of a noise; from 6 months on a baby might enjoy making noise on purpose by banging her cup on the table. A 6-month-old will look to the floor to search for a dropped toy. By 9 months, babies enjoy taking things out of containers and putting them back, solving simple manipulative problems, and discovering the consequences of their behavior.	Encourage infants' curiosity and exploration by playing games such as peekaboo. From 3 months on, provide an increasing variety of safe and interesting toys to manipulate. By 9 months, babies will enjoy everyday objects such as pots and pans, wooden spoons, and cardboard boxes of different sizes. Describe babies' play to them, and frequently narrate your interactions, as well.
Crying is a newborn baby's main method of communication, but by 3 months a baby smiles and makes a variety of sounds. At 3 to 6 months, *(cont.)*	Listen to babies, and respond. In the first few weeks, primary caregivers learn to differentiate a baby's cries—some mean hunger, while some *(cont.)*

What children are like	How adults can help
an infant listens attentively, coos, whimpers, gurgles, and laughs. From birth on, infants respond to voices; but by 6 months, babies respond to different voice tones and inflections. Six- to 9-month-olds gain more control over the sounds they produce; they can imitate tones and inflections to make a variety of sounds to express their feelings. By 9 months, babies may have a few early words such as "mama" and "dada," and are more responsive in conversation. They may carry out simple commands and repeat sequences of sounds. By now, babies do not always cry when displeased—they may yell!	indicate discomfort or other feelings. Tell babies what is happening as it happens, and prepare them for what is coming next. Respond to coos, smiles, and other communication, and allow time for babies to respond back. Sing to babies, and encourage them to experiment with things that make noise. By 6 months, babies will enjoy cloth or cardboard books; read to babies while snuggling them on your lap, and allow them to play with and manipulate books. At 9 months babies appreciate a greater variety of picture books, and are more aware of and sensitive to conversation, including with other infants. Talk to them and encourage their use of sounds and first words, and ask questions they can respond to.
Social development	
Babies are attracted to faces from birth on. They find them soothing, and even in the first weeks will make eye contact and may smile. Babies respond well to being held and have a strong need for it, especially in the first few weeks after birth. At 3 months, an infant displays clear signs of recognition for his primary caregiver, and will respond differently to different people. A 6-month-old baby may respond with fear to strangers and call to his primary caregiver for help. By 9 months, fear of strangers has intensified, and babies show clear preferences for their primary caregivers and are strongly attached to them.	Ensure that each infant identifies with a primary caregiver, and provide for frequent close contact with this special person. During the first few months, babies need minimal stimulation, which is met through interactions with caregivers and other children. Give infants time to look at people's faces, especially those of their primary caregivers.

What children are like	How adults can help
Infants need attentive care and interactions with adults who respond to their communicative sounds and promptly tend to their needs. They also enjoy and benefit from interacting with other infants. Infants' communication skills grow rapidly and inform these interactions with others. At 3 months, a baby will coo and babble when talked to; by 6 months, she can respond to her name and enjoy playing games such as peekaboo. At 9 months, babies are becoming more sensitive to others and are interested in their moods and activities; they may also tease. During the first nine months, babies learn to perform simple requests when asked and to anticipate events.	As babies grow, adapt their environment to encourage social interactions with adults and other children while also providing for their safety. A large playpen can hold both adult and child and will protect infants from more mobile toddlers. Communicate with babies, especially during caregiving routines, and respond to their coos and babbles with positive feedback. From 3 months on, play simple sound games with infants; babies 6 months and older will enjoy peekaboo and having caregivers copy their actions. Ask 9-month-olds simple questions or requests, and provide enough of a schedule for children to anticipate the sequence of events. Help children interpret the consequences of their behavior when it is safe to do so, and the effect their actions have on others.

Emotional development

Newborns do not differentiate themselves from the rest of the world. By 3 months, infants begin to realize that their hands and feet belong to them; this is the beginning of self-awareness. They begin to explore their body parts, using their hands to explore their eyes, mouth, and face in general. From 6 months on, a baby is increasingly aware of her body parts and the difference between herself and the rest of the world. A 9-month-old has enough awareness and control over her body to feed herself a teething biscuit and drink from a cup, and will enjoy the independence of doing things herself.	Help babies become self-aware by naming their body parts and commenting on their self-explorations ("You've caught your foot!"). From birth on, call infants by their names. Place them on their backs to see and hear the world and use their hands. Allow babies to explore and develop at their own pace, and provide opportunities to see, touch, and gum objects without forcing anything on them. By 6 months, children may be able to take over some self-help skills, and 9-month-olds may be able to use a spoon and hold a cup by the handle. Encourage children to problem solve and to do things by themselves when they can.

What children are like	How adults can help
From birth on, babies need to bond and form attachments with the special people in their lives who care for them. Consistent and responsive attention from these primary caregivers provides children with a sense of emotional security and well-being. Parents are usually the primary attachment figures, but babies also form strong attachments to others who care for them, such as child care professionals. Babies show attachment to their caregivers by calling out and reaching for them and crying when separated. A baby may start showing separation anxiety as early as 6 months, and by 9 months children show clear attachment to a primary caregiver and may fear separation.	Provide for babies' attachment needs by assigning a consistent caregiver. Newborns and very young infants need to be where they're safe and secure and their needs are easily met; they will need to be held much of the time. They may also need to be wrapped tightly in a blanket and placed in an enclosed space such as a bassinet when necessary to provide a sense of security. From 6 months on, primary caregivers may need to provide extra reassurance to children in the presence of strangers. Games such as peekaboo will help children learn that people can go and come back. By 9 months, caregivers can work with children to express, accept, and deal with separation fears.
Newborns show satisfaction or dissatisfaction by crying and making other sounds, as well as through expressions and movements. They are soothed by looking at faces, as well as by being held and cared for tenderly. By 3 months, infants show a wider variety of feelings and by now will smile. Six-month-olds have a larger emotional range and develop individual taste preferences. By now, babies may assert some independence by starting to self-feed. From this point on, children's individual personalities begin to show, which color their emotional responses to people and situations. By 9 months, they will show clear preferences by rejecting things they don't want.	Caregivers should respond to infants' messages and try to determine their real needs. Adults learn to interpret infants' cries, help comfort them, and help them to comfort themselves. Adults should hold infants during feedings, and let babies have enough time looking at their faces. Caregivers should recognize and respect children's feelings, and help them process emotions by discussing what they seem to express, especially during caregiving routines. By 9 months, caregivers should take care to provide positive models for children by expressing honest feelings, and provide opportunities for children to assert themselves and express preferences.

Children ages 8–18 months

What children are like	How adults can help
Physical development	
By 9 months, babies have gained enough control and mobility to roll from front to back, sit up, and make progress toward crawling. Infants are becoming mobile; rolling, creeping, and crawling soon leads to pulling up to standing and cruising around the room while holding onto furniture. A 12-month-old can often stand without holding on, and may walk but probably still prefers to crawl. Toddlers learn to climb up and down stairs, and may climb out of a crib. At 18 months, toddlers can walk fast and will seldom fall. They can now run awkwardly, and can walk up stairs while holding an adult's hand.	Provide open spaces and safe climbing opportunities both indoors and outdoors for children to enjoy crawling and climbing, and to practice walking. As children gain mobility, create challenges by adding pillows, low furniture, and other safe materials to make different levels to climb and pull up on. Help children who can stand but can't get back down, but promote their problem solving. Playpens should be large enough for adult caregivers to join children. As toddlers learn to walk, provide for their safety and offer plenty of opportunities for movement. Don't push children to walk—allow them to decide when they are finished with crawling. By 18 months, toddlers need room to walk and run; they will enjoy taking walks that aren't too goal-oriented. Allow children to practice new skills repetitively if they want.
By 9 months, babies have gained control in grasping, manipulating, and exploring objects. They now can use their thumbs and forefingers in a pincer grip to pick up even very small objects. At 12 months old, children can use their thumbs well, show preference for one hand, and may use both hands at the same time for different things. They may be able to undress themselves or untie shoes, and can use an index finger to point at objects. By 18 months, toddlers can scribble with crayons and imitate marks, and have more control while self-feeding.	Encourage use of manipulative skills, such as pulling off socks, opening doors, and taking apart nesting toys. Children can pick up very small objects and will put them in their mouths, so adults must monitor the environment closely for anything dangerous. Offer mobile infants small finger foods such as dry cereal and cooked peas, and provide lots of objects to manipulate, explore, experiment with, and carry around. Offer children plenty of sensory experiences such as water and sand play.

8–18 months, cont.

What children are like	How adults can help
Intellectual development	
By 9 months, babies remember games and toys from previous days, anticipate a person's return, and can concentrate for periods of time without interruption. They enjoy taking things out of containers and putting them back, solving simple manipulative problems, discovering the consequences of their behavior, and doing things over and over again. Mobile infants have increased memory and gain the understanding that out-of-sight people and objects still exist; they are now good at finding hidden objects. They enjoy using trial-and-error and exploring new approaches to problems, and can even sometimes think about their actions ahead of time. By 18 months, children can begin to solve problems in their heads.	Allow babies space to explore the environment and interact with others. Provide everyday objects such as pots and pans, wooden spoons, and different sized boxes as well as manipulative toys such as large beads to string, large LEGO™ blocks, building blocks, and stacking toys. Provide a variety of experiences, and talk about them with children. By 18 months, children will enjoy choosing their own toys from a variety displayed on low shelves. Toys such as small figurines, animals, doll houses, containers, and measuring cups are good options. Offer toddlers choices of activities, and give them uninterrupted time to play and work on problems.
From 9 months to a year old, babies communicate with a variety of sounds and a few early words such as "mama" and "dada." They can understand and carry out simple commands, repeat sequences of sounds, and often will yell instead of cry. By 12 months, children learn that words stand for objects. They are beginning to use the same sounds and intonations as their parents, can use gestures to express themselves, and may now say two to eight words. Mobile infants' language development	Talk frequently with toddlers and give them simple commands to follow during daily routines. Encourage interactions between children, and involve them in groups or one-on-one in simple games. Ask children questions, and encourage them to ask questions too. Describe activities to children, narrating the actions of both adults and children. Introduce a greater variety of picture books, and frequently read aloud to children. By 18 months, introduce books with clear, simple pictures. Encourage
(cont.)	*(cont.)*

What children are like	How adults can help
increases rapidly; by 18 months, children may know 10 words and may use them to gain attention and to indicate wants. Children throughout this age become increasingly interested in picture books.	children's use of sounds and first words, and ask questions they can respond to. Name the things children point at, fill in missing words, and expand utterances for children. Caregivers can also sing songs, do finger plays, and expose children to music.
By 12 months, children start playing with toys and household objects in more sophisticated ways. They can now imitate people who are not present and mimic adult behavior. By 18 months, mobile infants have made the mental leaps necessary for pretend play, and can now begin to fantasize and role-play.	Offer children toys that provide reasons to talk, such as telephones and dolls. Return dramatic play toys and props to a designated space for children to find, while allowing them to play with the materials wherever they would like. Model basic pretend play with children and interact with them.
Social development	
Almost all mobile infants will show some wariness or even intense fear of strangers. They have clear preferences for their primary caregivers, whom they are strongly attached to. Infants' conversations with adults become more reciprocal as they organize sounds into expressive jargon that approximates sentences. They are learning about others' moods and activities, and during this time children become increasingly interested in peers. They may choose a favorite friend to follow or imitate, and may smile and babble at other children. However, they will often still treat peers like objects.	Maintain strong, loving relationships in order to offer mobile infants a secure base for exploration. Respond to their sounds and early words, and ask them questions they can respond to. Provide for interaction with other children while ensuring they do not accidentally hurt each other, and help them interpret the effect of their actions on others.

What children are like	How adults can help
In addition to physical contact, eye contact, vocalizing, and gesturing become increasingly important for maintaining connections with those children love and trust. However, children in this age range are eager to explore and to take their first physical and emotional steps toward independence. Mobile infants can now feed themselves and are interested in the dressing process. They can obey commands and seek adults' approval, but they are also learning to say no and may not always be cooperative.	Continue to foster a spirit of cooperation and partnership by involving each child as a partner in daily routines such as feeding, diapering, dressing, washing, and grooming. However, expect some uncooperativeness as the push toward independence arises. For example, when a child rolls over during diapering, cooperate with the child by moving to where she is. Continue to use language to maintain connections with children while they become more independent. Foster problem solving and promote self-help skills by providing needed tools, equipment, and encouragement. Set limits when necessary and gently but firmly enforce them, and allow children to discover the consequences of their behavior when it is safe to do so.
Mobile infants become increasingly interested in the world of adults, and can imitate adults in dramatic play. They are interested in real-life actions and enjoy helping with chores, and are learning some social roles and manners such as waving "bye-bye." They may also start gaining some bladder and bowel control. Children are learning to respond to their own names and to recognize names of other people and objects.	Help children learn important names by repeating names of people, objects, and actions in their environment. Encourage and provide materials for dramatic play, such as dress-up clothes, dolls, and housekeeping equipment. Continue to provide consistency and enough of a schedule for children to begin anticipating the sequence of events, and allow children to help out with classroom routines as they are able.

What children are like	How adults can help
Emotional development	
Children at this stage have very powerful feelings, and new fears come with their increased mobility. Mobile infants are clearly attached to their primary caregivers and may fear separation, along with strangers and new places. Unfamiliar sights and people may be terrifying, and transitions such as drop-off and pickup may be difficult. A child may need a "lovey," such as a blanket or stuffed toy, as a source of emotional stability. Children will show affection toward their caregivers, and still need them to be a reassuring base for their explorations.	Remember that mobile infants still need the security of trusted adults, and provide for children's need for continuity of care and attachment to a primary caregiver as much as possible. Provide comfort and reassurance when children are frightened by unfamiliar things or people, and help children express, accept, and deal with separation fears. Provide protected areas in the environment for quiet play to avoid overstimulation. Offer approval, give and return affection, and play games such as peekaboo that show people can go and come back.
Mobile infants will reject things they don't want and learn to say no to assert independence. They show a wide variety of emotions and respond to those of others, gradually developing the understanding that others have their own experiences and feelings. Children may now know the difference between their possessions and those of others. They will show moods and preferences, which they may indicate with simple gestures such as pointing or shaking their heads.	Provide the opportunity for mobile infants to become assertive, as well as tools and plenty of opportunities to develop self-help skills. Accept uncooperative behavior and use of the word no as signs of self-assertion, but respect and communicate with families whose cultures differ in beliefs about infants' independence. Adults should be good role models for children in expressing honest feelings, and offer words for emotions. Learn some words of affection in the home language of dual-language learners. Acknowledge infants' possessions and help protect them, and talk children through aggressive situations. Set reasonable limits, and offer choices.

Children ages 16–36 months

What children are like	How adults can help
Physical development	
Toddlers are busy tackling new gross motor skills, building on confidence gained by mastering walking. They learn to jump, tiptoe, march, throw and kick a ball, and make a riding toy go by pushing with their feet. They're excited by their new motor abilities and plunge ahead before figuring out how to stop. A 24-month-old will still likely need to hold on up and down stairs and may have trouble stopping and turning while running. By 36 months, children's skills are quite developed—they can run with control, throw a ball with aim, jump in place, briefly balance on one foot, and may even pedal a tricycle.	Provide toddlers with plenty of freedom, opportunity, and choice in physical exercise, within appropriate limits. Encourage children to find new ways to combine and use familiar toys and equipment, and keep the environment interesting with periodic changes. By 24 months, offer equipment such as low climbers and slides; large balls (both lightweight and heavier); large, lightweight blocks; riding vehicles designed for toddlers (with pedals and without); and swings children can get into and out of themselves. Offer an environment with features such as hills, ramps, low stairs, and open space. Include movement and songs during circle time, but don't make group times compulsory. Allow roughhousing done in a loving spirit, while preventing children from unintentionally hurting each other. By 36 months, provide some larger gross motor equipment, including outside pieces for more boisterous play. As toddlers' physical skills mature, provide them with access to preschool equipment to prepare for their transition out of the toddler program. They may now enjoy materials such as large wooden blocks, balance boards, planks, boxes, and ladders for building. Be sure to offer both boys and girls equal encouragement in physical activities; girls may need more if they are reluctant.

What children are like	How adults can help
Toddlers enjoy sensory experiences and experimenting with art materials such as scribbling with crayons and markers. They gain fine motor control while self-feeding—by 24 months, toddlers can hold a spoon, fork, and cup (although they may still spill). Children can now use a paintbrush, although they can't control drips. They can turn pages of a sturdy board book, and put on some easy clothing. Toddlers love playing with sand and water and experimenting with different textures. By 36 months, they may be able to put on their own clothing (except for buttoning) and shoes (except for tying laces). Toddlers can now scribble with more control and can draw a circle, use a paintbrush while controlling drips, and manipulate toys more creatively. Older toddlers can also exercise bowel and bladder control.	Stimulate children's fine motor skills with a variety of sensory experiences and opportunities for play with manipulatives. Offer sand and water to explore, as well as art materials such as crayons and markers. Keep in mind that some materials such as playdough, paint, and toys with small parts may not be appropriate for young toddlers. Likewise, avoid using food items as manipulatives, as toddlers are still learning what cannot be eaten. By 24 months, offer materials such as wooden puzzles with several large pieces, pegboards, stacking toys, big beads to string, easy-to-put-together construction sets, playdough, rhythm instruments, texture matching games, feely boxes, toys to play with in sand and water, dolls to dress and undress, and sturdy books with enticing features. Offer older toddlers more complex toys, such as a flannel board set or unit blocks with accompanying accessories. Model use of art materials and tools such as safety scissors and glue for older toddlers, and find ways for older children to engage in fine motor manipulative activities without interruption by younger children who would rather dump than build. Encourage fine motor activities in both boys and girls, and if boys are less interested, entice them with engaging materials.

What children are like	How adults can help
Intellectual development	
Toddlers' memory, problem-solving, and overall cognitive skills are rapidly developing. Every stage of motor development involves solving problems as children deal with gravity, learn to balance, and explore how to use their muscles and joints. When children struggle to reach the next developmental stage, they are problem solving. They also solve problems such as how to get a particular toy or other object, which relates to social problem solving when someone else has it. By 18 months they begin to solve problems in their heads, and by 24 months they can solve even more complex problems. Toddlers' problem solving becomes increasingly sophisticated as they approach 36 months. They love to sort by categories, can work simple puzzles and fit shapes into a form board, compare sizes, and may learn to count to 2 or 3. Toddlers enjoy learning about themselves and others, and develop an understanding of who they are. Toddlers learn whether they are boys or girls and can identify most parts of the body. Older toddlers may be able to draw a face, or even a very simple figure.	Toddlers need choices of activities and plenty of time and encouragement for play and problem solving. Offer a variety of toys that allow choices and provide opportunities for concept development and problem solving, such as puzzles, figurines and toy animals, dolls and dollhouses, containers, and measuring cups. Involve children with materials and activities such as constructing a simple collage or piecing together parquetry blocks, and allow them to concentrate undisturbed while they are absorbed in their activities. Encourage creative thinking and an inquiring attitude and offer simple, hands-on science displays and experiments, as well as experiences that foster development of number and other math concepts in a natural context. Help children learn about themselves and others, and encourage expressions of feelings and verbal conflict resolution.

What children are like	How adults can help
Toddlers' communication skills grow by leaps and bounds during this age period. By 18 months, children may know 10 words; by 24 months they can use two- and three-word sentences and their vocabulary has increased to as many as 50 to 200 words. By 36 months, children may have a 900-word vocabulary and can articulate fairly clearly. Children are increasingly interested in books and can name pictures and label actions. Toddlers learn to use personal pronouns (I, me, you) and refer to themselves by name. By 36 months, children can use language to convey simple ideas and information, and can converse in short sentences and answer questions. Some dual-language learners can sometimes do all of the above in two languages.	Provide a variety of books, and model how to use them carefully. Read aloud to children, and discuss illustrations. Post pictures at children's eye level around the room and change them often—these will give children something to talk about. Encourage conversation between children and between children and adults, and help children begin to talk out differences instead of relying on hitting, kicking, and other negative physical behaviors. Prompt children to discuss places they've been, and arrange for experiences that give children something to talk about. Embed language throughout the day; tell stories, sing songs, and provide for other music experiences.
Toddlers' ability for abstract thought becomes more developed during this age period. Through play, they develop increasingly complex mental representations of the real world. Adults are favorite play partners, as they can maintain and enrich the play's storyline with language and ideas not yet mastered by the toddler. Play with peers also becomes increasingly interactive, and partners or small groups may work together or take on simple pretend play roles. Toddlers love to repeat favorite stories over and over again in their play and may reenact events they have participated in or seen.	Participate in and model dramatic play, but respond to the children's lead. Provide toys such as stuffed animals, figurines, and small vehicles for children to play with. Enrich play by adding missing words or new elements, but support toddlers' needs to repeat the same story many times. Help children imagine and speculate ("I wonder what would happen if . . ."), and encourage verbalization of feelings and wants. Older toddlers will be able to think about past experiences as well as future ones; talk to them about what they remember and what they might predict may happen.

What children are like	How adults can help
Social development	
Toddlers' developing sense of self is informed by their desire and drive for independence and control. Their growing social awareness imparts cultural messages about who they are and how they should be. Children in this age range still need the security of warm and close relationships with special adults, but their desire to explore intensifies. As they assert their independence, they are learning about the differences between themselves and others. Children learn how to use personal pronouns (I, me, you) and refer to themselves by name. They also gradually start to understand personal property concepts ("That's mine," "That's Daddy's").	Help toddlers find appropriate ways to assert themselves by supporting their individuality and offering choices whenever possible. Introduce social guidelines, setting limits and gently but firmly enforcing them. Provide a well designed environment that offers children many chances to be in control as they participate in group play, fantasy play, and independent activities. Recognize that the values families place on self-help skills and independence vary from culture to culture, and discuss parent's feelings and ideas about self-direction and how teachers help the children.
Toddlers have much greater social awareness than do infants, and will now actively seek out friends. They are fascinated by their own bodies and others'. They enjoy imitating others' behavior and learn to conform to a group for short periods of time. Toddlers enjoy simple interactive group activities such as "follow the leader" or singing songs. Children will seek out friends with similar interests and will develop affections and attachments for peers. Throughout this age period children gradually gain some regard for others' possessions; while a 24-month-old will commonly hoard favorite toys, a 36-month-old may share.	Promote interactions among children, and help them understand how they are seen by others and consider how their actions affect one another. Respect children's need to hold on to their possessions, and minimize conflicts by providing space for personal possessions (cubbies or boxes). Model, rather than require, sharing, and offer duplicates of favorite toys and choices of activities so it isn't such an issue. Begin to encourage sharing and cooperative play in older toddlers, and involve children in short, active group sessions such as circle time.

What children are like	How adults can help
Toddlers are fascinated by the actions of adults and the world around them; they will imitate adults in dramatic play and are interested in helping with chores. They have a strong need to reenact events through play in order to understand them. Toddlers are interested in the dressing process and may be able to participate to some extent. During this age period they gain bladder and bowel control, and by 36 months most are willing to use the toilet.	Support dramatic play, and provide materials such as dress-up clothes, dolls, housekeeping equipment, figurines, and toy vehicles. Encourage self-help skills and allow children to help as they are able and do things by themselves, even when you know you can do them better or faster. Discuss perspectives on toilet learning and readiness with parents. If you are in agreement, follow the child's lead in toilet learning, beginning when the toddler shows signs of interest and readiness. If you disagree with the family's approach, listen to parents and discuss together what to do about the child's toilet learning until you come to consensus.

Emotional development

Toddlers struggle to balance their desires for both independence and closeness—they are not yet "big kids," but are no longer babies. They want to assert their independence ("Me do it!") and may say no even to things they want. They take pride in accomplishments as they gain self-help skills and powers of concentration. At the same time, they may succumb to tantrums when overwhelmed by fatigue, anxiety, or other distress.	Support each child's growing identity by showing him how positively you see him. Help children understand how they affect others, and foster positive interactions. Set clear rules and limits for safety and provide consistent, yet flexible routines. Help children have accomplishments they can take pride in, and describe their actions positively ("You worked hard to finish the puzzle!") rather than with blanket praise ("Good job!"). Foster involvement and persistence in play activities by preventing interruptions by other children. Equip the care setting with materials that facilitate self-help skills, such as small pitchers and serving utensils or easy-to-put on smocks, and offer just enough help for children to be successful.

Basics of Developmentally Appropriate Practice

What children are like	How adults can help
Toddlers' sense of empathy develops as they begin to understand that others' feelings differ from their own. This often stems from conflict over strong feelings, commonly originating in struggles over possessions. Children may despair over not getting what they want or experiencing the displeasure of special adults. However, they respond equally strongly to warmth and generosity. They observe adult relationships and learn how to build strong, positive connections with others.	Encourage verbalization of feelings and talking through conflicts. Help children listen to one another, and talk them through aggressive situations. Explain how others may interpret a particular action or event. Provide dramatic play experiences and equipment that allows children to express their feelings, such as puppets. Offer other outlets for expression, such as art, music, and large muscle experiences. Read books with children that help them identify and express their feelings. Support each child, and model positive interactions and negotiations with fellow adults.

References

Baker, A.C., & L.A. Manfredi/Petitt. 2004. *Relationships, the heart of quality care: Creating community among adults in early care settings.* Washington, DC: NAEYC.

Bodrova, E., & D.J. Leong. 2003. Chopsticks and counting chips: Do play and foundational skills need to compete for the teacher's attention in an early childhood classroom? *Young Children* 58 (3): 10–17.

Bowman, B.T., M.S. Donovan & M.S. Burns, eds. 2000. *Eager to learn: Educating our preschoolers.* Washington, DC: National Academies Press. Available online: www. nap.edu.

Bronson, P., & A. Merryman. 2009. *NurtureShock: New thinking about children.* New York: Twelve.

Bronfenbrenner, U. 1979. *The ecology of human development: Experiments by nature and design.* Cambridge, MA: Harvard University Press.

California Dept. of Education & WestEd Center for Child and Family Studies. 2009. *California infant/toddler learning & development foundations.* Sacramento, CA: California Department of Education.

Copple, C., & S. Bredekamp, eds. 2009. *Developmentally appropriate practice in early childhood programs serving children from birth through age 8.* 3d ed. Washington, DC: NAEYC.

Davidson, J. 1996. *Emergent literacy and dramatic play in early education.* Albany, NY: Delmar.

Dodge, D.T., S. Rudick & K. Berke, et al. 2010. *The creative curriculum for infants, toddlers & twos.* 2d ed., rev. Washington, DC: Teaching Strategies.

Etzioni, A. 1996. *The new golden rule: Community and morality in a democratic society.* New York: Basic Books.

Galinsky, E. 2010. *Mind in the making: The seven essential life skills every child needs*. New York: HarperStudio.

Gestwicki, C. 2011. *Developmentally appropriate practice: Curriculum and development in early education*. 4th ed. Mason, OH: Wadsworth.

Gonzalez-Mena, J., & A. Stonehouse. 2008. *Making links: A collaborative approach to planning and practice in early childhood programs*. New York: Teachers College Press.

Gopnik, A. 2009. *The philosophical baby: What children's minds tell us about truth, love, and the meaning of life*. New York: Farrar, Straus and Giroux.

Hammond, R.A. 2009. *Respecting babies: A new look at Magda Gerber's RIE approach*. Washington, DC: Zero to Three.

Hart, C.H., D.C. Burts & R. Charlesworth. 1997. Integrated developmentally appropriate curriculum: From theory and research to practice. In *Integrated curriculum and developmentally appropriate practice*, eds. C. Hart, D. Burts & R. Charlesworth, 1–27. Albany, NY: State University of New York Press.

Hart, B., & T. Risley. 1995. *Meaningful differences in everyday parenting and intellectual development in young American children*. Baltimore, MD: Paul H. Brookes.

Honig, A.S. 2002. *Secure relationships: Nurturing infant/toddler attachment in early care settings*. Washington, DC: NAEYC.

Jablon, J.R., A.L. Dombro & M.L. Dichtelmiller. 2007. *The power of observation for birth through eight*. 2d ed. Washington, DC: Teaching Strategies; Washington, DC: NAEYC.

Jones, E. 1978. Teacher education: Entertainment or interaction? *Young Children* 33 (3): 15–23.

Jones, E., & G. Reynolds. 1992. *The play's the thing: Teachers' roles in children's play*. New York: Teachers College Press.

Kostelnik, M.J., A.K. Soderman & A.P. Whiren. 1999. *Developmentally appropriate curriculum: Best practices in early childhood education*. 2d ed. Upper Saddle River, NJ: Prentice Hall.

Lally, J.R. 1995. The impact of child care policies and practices on infant/toddler identity formation. *Young Children* 51 (1): 58–67.

Lally, J.R. 2009. The science and psychology of infant–toddler care: How an understanding of early learning has transformed child care. *Zero to Three* 30 (2): 47–53.

Marulis, L.M. 2000. Anti-bias teaching to address cultural diversity. *Multicultural Education* 7 (3): 27–31.

McAfee, O., D.J. Leong & E. Bodrova. 2004. *Basics of assessment: A primer for early childhood educators*. Washington, DC: NAEYC.

NAEYC. 2005. Screening and assessment of young English-language learners. Supplement to the NAEYC Position Statement on Early Childhood Curriculum, Assessment, and Program Evaluation. Washington, DC: Author. Also online: www.naeyc.org/positionstatements.

NAEYC. 2007. *NAEYC Early Childhood Program Standards and Accreditation Criteria: The mark of quality in early childhood education*. Washington, DC: Author. Also online: www.naeyc.org/academy.

NAEYC. 2009. Developmentally appropriate practice in early childhood programs serving children from birth through age 8. Position Statement. Washington, DC: Author. Also online: www.naeyc.org/positionstatements.

NAEYC & NAECS/SDE (National Association of Early Childhood Specialists in State Departments of Education). 2003. Early childhood curriculum, assessment, and program evaluation: Building an effective, accountable system in programs for children birth to age 8. Joint Position Statement. Washington, DC: Author. Also online: www.naeyc.org/positionstatements.

Odom, L.L., R. Wolery, J. Lieber & E. Horn. 2002. *Widening the circle: Including children with disabilities in preschool programs*. New York: Teachers College Press.

Ong, F., & T. Cole, eds. 2009. *Inclusion works! Creating child care programs that promote belonging for children with special needs*. Sacramento, CA: California Dept. of Education.

Petersen, S.H., & D.S. Wittmer. 2009. *Endless opportunities for infant and toddler curriculum: A relationship-based approach*. Upper Saddle River, NJ: Pearson.

Piaget, J. 1952. *The origins of intelligence in children*. New York: International Universities Press.

Pianta, R.C. 2000. *Enhancing relationships between children and teachers*. Washington, DC: American Psychological Association.

Post, J., M. Hohmann & A.S. Epstein. 2011. *Tender care and early learning: Supporting infants and toddlers in child care settings*. 2d ed. Ypsilanti, MI: HighScope Press.

Raikes, H.H., & C.P. Edwards. 2009. *Extending the dance in infant and toddler caregiving: Enhancing attachment and relationships*. Baltimore, MD: Paul H. Brookes; Washington, DC: NAEYC.

Sandall, S., M.E. McLean & B.J. Smith. 2000. *DEC recommended practices in early intervention/early childhood special education*. Denver, CO: Division for Early Childhood (DEC) of the Council for Exceptional Children (CEC).

Sawyers, J.K., & C.S. Rogers. 1988. *Helping young children develop through play.* Washington, DC: NAEYC.

Schweinhart, L.J., & D.P. Weikart. 1997. The High/Scope preschool curriculum comparison study through age 23. *Early Childhood Research Quarterly* 12 (2).

Shonkoff, J.P., & D.A. Phillips, eds. 2000. *From neurons to neighborhoods: The science of early childhood development.* Washington, DC: National Academies Press. Also online: www.nap.edu.

Smilansky, S. 1990. Sociodramatic play: Its relevance to behavior and achievement in schools. In *Children's play and learning: Perspectives and policy implications*, eds. E. Klugman & S. Smilansky, 18–42. New York: Teachers College Press.

Stechuk, R.A., M.S. Burns & S.E. Yandian. 2006. *Bilingual infant/toddler environments: Supporting language and learning in our youngest children.* Washington, DC: Academy for Educational Development.

Stone, J.G. 2001. *Building classroom community: The early childhood teacher's role.* Washington, DC: NAEYC.

Tabors, P.O. 2008. *One child, two languages: A guide for early childhood educators of children learning English as a second language.* 2d ed. Baltimore, MD: Paul H. Brookes.

Tardos, A., ed. 2007. *Bringing up and providing care for infants and toddlers in an institution.* Budapest, Hungary: Pikler-LoczyTarsasag.

Tough, P. 2009. *Whatever it takes: Geoffrey Canada's quest to change Harlem and America.* New York: Mariner Books.

U.S. Dept. of Health and Human Services. 2006, April. *Early Head Start benefits children and families.* Washington, DC: Administration for Children and Families, Office of Planning, Research and Evaluation, Head Start Bureau. Also online: http://www.acf.hhs.gov/programs/opre/ehs/ehs_resrch/reports/dissemination/research_briefs/research_brief_overall.pdf

Vygotsky, L.S. [1934] 1986. *Thought and language.* Cambridge, MA: MIT Press.

Zero to Three. 2008. *Caring for infants and toddlers in groups: Developmentally appropriate practice.* 2d ed. Washington, DC: Zero to Three.

Resources

Print

Alati, S. 2005. What about our passions as teachers? Incorporating individual interests in emergent curricula. *Young Children* 60 (6): 86–89.

American Academy of Pediatrics, American Public Health Association & National Resource Center for Health and Safety in Child Care and Early Education. 2011. *Caring for our children—National health and safety performance standards: Guidelines for early care and education programs.* 3d ed. Elk Grove Village, IL: American Academy of Pediatrics; Washington, DC: American Public Health Association.

Aronson, S.S., ed. 2002. *Healthy young children: A manual for programs.* 4th ed. Washington, DC: NAEYC.

Bardige, B.S., & M.M. Segal. 2005. *Building literacy with love: A guide for teachers and caregivers of children birth through age 5.* Washington, DC: Zero to Three.

Berk, L. 2004. *Infants and children: Prenatal through middle childhood.* 5th ed. Boston, MA: Allyn and Bacon.

Bowman, B., ed. 2002. *Love to read.* Washington, DC: National Black Child Development Institute.

Birckmayer, J., A. Kennedy & A. Stonehouse. 2009. Using stories effectively with infants and toddlers. *Young Children* 64 (1): 42–47.

Bronson, M.B. 1995. *The right stuff for children birth to 8: Selecting play materials to support development.* Washington, DC: NAEYC.

Burns, M.S., P. Griffin & C.E. Snow, eds. 1999. *Starting out right: A guide to promoting children's reading success.* Washington, DC: National Academies Press. Also online: www.nap.edu.

Butterfield, P.M., C.A. Martin & A.P. Prairie. 2004. *Emotional connections: How relationships guide early learning.* Washington, DC: Zero to Three.

Carlebach, D., & B. Tate. 2002. *Creating caring children: The first three years.* Miami, FL: Peace Education Foundation.

Copple, C., & S. Bredekamp, eds. 2009. *Developmentally appropriate practice in early childhood programs serving children from birth through age 8.* 3d ed. Washington, DC: NAEYC.

David, M., & G. Appell. 2001. *Loczy: An unusual approach to mothering.* Budapest, Hungary: LoczyTarsasag.

Davidson, J. 1996. *Emerging literacy and dramatic play in early education.* Albany, NY: Delmar.

Day, C.B., ed. 2004. *Essentials for child development associates working with young children.* Washington, DC: Council for Professional Recognition.

Derman-Sparks, L., & J. Olsen Edwards. 2010. *Anti-bias education for young children and ourselves.* Washington, DC: NAEYC.

Dickinson, D.K., & P.O. Tabors. 2001. *Beginning literacy with language: Young children learning at home and school.* Baltimore, MD: Paul H. Brookes.

Diffily, D., & K. Morrison, eds. 1996. *Family-friendly communication for early childhood programs.* Washington, DC: NAEYC.

Dodge, D.T., L.J. Colker & C. Heroman. 2000. *Connecting content, teaching, and learning.* Washington, DC: Teaching Strategies.

Dunn, L., & S. Kontos. 1997. What have we learned about developmentally appropriate practice? *Young Children* 52 (5): 4–13.

Eggers-Piérola, C. 2005. *Connections and commitments: Reflecting Latino values in early childhood programs.* Portsmouth, NH: Heinemann.

Egley, E.H., & R.J. Egley. 2000. Teaching principals, parents, and colleagues about developmentally appropriate practice. *Young Children* 55 (5): 48–51.

Espinosa, L.M. 2010. *Getting it RIGHT for young children from diverse backgrounds: Applying research to improve practice.* Boston, MA: Pearson.

Falk, B. 2000. *The heart of the matter: Using standards and assessment to learn.* Portsmouth, NH: Heinemann.

Falk, J. 2007. The importance of person-oriented adult-child relationships and its basic conditions. In *Bringing up and providing care for infants and toddlers in an institution,* ed. A. Tardos, 23–37. Budapest, Hungary: Pikler-LoczyTarsasag.

Galinsky, E. 2010. *Mind in the making: The seven essential life skills every child needs.* New York: HarperStudio.

Gartrell, D. 2004. *The power of guidance: Teaching social-emotional skills in early childhood classrooms.* Clifton Park, NY: Thomson Delmar Learning; Washington, DC: NAEYC.

Genishi, C., & A.H. Dyson. 2009. *Children, language, and literacy: Diverse learners in diverse times.* New York: Teachers College Press; Washington, DC: NAEYC.

Gestwicki, C. 2011. *Developmentally appropriate practice: Curriculum and development in early education.* 4th ed. Mason, OH: Wadsworth.

Gonzalez-Mena, J. 2008. *Diversity in early care and education: Honoring differences.* 5th ed. New York: McGraw-Hill; Washington, DC: NAEYC.

Gonzalez-Mena, J. 2010. *50 Strategies for communicating and working with diverse families.* 2d ed. Boston, MA: Pearson.

Gonzalez-Mena, J., & A. Stonehouse. 2008. *Making links: A collaborative approach to planning and practice in early childhood programs.* New York: Teachers College Press.

Gonzalez-Mena, J., & D.W. Eyer. 2009. *Infants, toddlers, and caregivers.* 8th ed. New York: McGraw-Hill.

Gopnik, A. 2009. *The philosophical baby: What children's minds tell us about truth, love, and the meaning of life.* New York: Farrar, Straus and Giroux.

Hannaford, C. 2007. *Smart moves: Why learning is not all in your head.* 2d ed. Salt Lake City, UT: Great River.

Hammond, R.A. 2009. *Respecting babies: A new look at Magda Gerber's RIE approach.* Washington, DC: Zero to Three.

Heroman, C., & C. Jones. 2004. *Literacy: The Creative Curriculum approach.* Washington, DC: Teaching Strategies.

Hirsch, E. 1996. *The block book.* 3d ed. Washington, DC: NAEYC.

Howes, C. 2010. *Culture and child development in early childhood programs: Practices for quality education and care.* New York: Teachers College Press.

IRA (International Reading Association) & NAEYC. 1998. *Learning to read and write: Developmentally appropriate practices for young children.* Joint Position Statement. Washington, DC: NAEYC. Online: www.naeyc.org/positionstatements. Also in Neuman, Copple & Bredekamp 2000.

Jablon, J.R., A.L. Dombro & M.L. Dichtelmiller. 2007. *The power of observation for birth through eight.* 2d ed. Washington, DC: Teaching Strategies; Washington, DC: NAEYC.

Jalongo, M.R. 2004. *Young children and picture books.* 2d ed. Washington, DC: NAEYC.

Kaiser, B., & J.S. Rasminsky. 1999. *Meeting the challenge: Effective strategies for challenging behaviours in early childhood environments.* Ottawa, ONT: Canadian Child Care Federation.

Kallo, E., & G. Balog. 2005. *The origins of free play.* Budapest, Hungary: Pikler-Loczy-Tarsasag.

Keyser, J. 2006. *From parents to partners: Building a family-centered program.* St. Paul, MN: Redleaf; Washington, DC: NAEYC.

Koralek, D.G., ed. 2005. Developmentally appropriate practice in 2005: Updates from the field. Special issue. *Young Children* 60 (4).

Kovach, B., & D.D. Ros-Voseles. 2008. *Being with babies: Understanding and responding to the infants in your care.* Beltsville, MD: Gryphon House.

Lally, J.R. 1995. The impact of child care policies and practices on infant/toddler identity formation. *Young Children* 51 (1): 58–67.

Lally, J.R., & P. Mangione. 2006. The uniqueness of infancy demands a responsive approach to care. *Young Children* 61 (4): 14–20.

Landry, S.H. 2005. *Effective early childhood programs: Turning knowledge into action.* Houston, TX: University of Texas, Health Science Center.

McAfee, O., D.J. Leong & E. Bodrova. 2004. *Basics of assessment: A primer for early childhood educators.* Washington, DC: NAEYC.

McMullen, M.B., J.M. Addleman, A.M. Fulford, S.L. Moore, S.J. Mooney, S.S. Sisk & J. Zachariah. 2009. Learning to be me while coming to understand we: Encouraging prosocial babies in group settings. *Young Children* 64 (4): 20–28.

Meier, D.R. 2004.*The young child's memory for words: Developing first and second language and literacy.* New York: Teachers College Press.

Meisels, S.J., & E.S. Fenichel, eds. 1996. *New visions for the developmental assessment of infants and young children.* Washington, DC: Zero to Three/National Center for Infants, Toddlers, and Families.

Miller, K. 2001. *Ages and stages: Developmental descriptions and activities, birth through eight years.* Rev. ed. West Palm Beach, FL: Telshare.

Money, R. 2006. *Unfolding of infants' natural gross motor development.* Los Angeles, CA: Resources for Infant Educarers.

Mooney, C.G. 2010. *Theories of attachment: An introduction to Bowlby, Ainsworth, Gerber, Brazelton, Kennell, and Klaus.* St. Paul, MN: Redleaf.

NAEYC. 2005. *Self-study kit for program quality improvement.* Washington, DC: Author. [Available from the NAEYC Academy for Early Childhood Program Accreditation: www.naeyc.org.]

Neuman, S.B., C. Copple & S. Bredekamp. 2000. *Learning to read and write: Developmentally appropriate practices for young children.* Washington, DC: NAEYC.

Owocki, G. 2001. *Make way for literacy: Teaching the way young children learn.* Portsmouth, NH: Heinemann; Washington, DC: NAEYC.

Petrie, S., & S. Owen, eds. 2005. *Authentic relationships in group care for infants and toddlers—Resources for infant educarers (RIE) principles into practice.* London: J. Kingsley.

Pica, R. 2010. Learning by leaps and bounds: Babies on the move. *Young Children* 65 (4): 48, 50.

Rushton, S.P. 2001. Applying brain research to create developmentally appropriate learning environments. *Young Children* 56 (5): 76–82.

Sandall, S., M.E. McLean & B.J. Smith. 2000. *DEC recommended practices in early intervention/early childhood special education.* Denver, CO: Division for Early Childhood (DEC) of the Council for Exceptional Children (CEC).

Schickedanz, J. 1999. *Much more than the ABCs: The early stages of reading and writing.* Washington, DC: NAEYC.

Seiderman, E. 2009. Family support builds stronger families: The roots of family-supportive child care. *Exchange* 186 (Mar-Apr): 66–69.

Siegel, D.J. 1999. *The developing mind: How relationships and the brain interact to shape who we are.* New York: Guilford.

Shonkoff, J.P., & D.A. Phillips, eds. 2000. *From neurons to neighborhoods: The science of early childhood development.* Washington, DC: National Academies Press. Also online: www.nap.edu.

Smilansky, S. 1990. Sociodramatic play: Its relevance to behavior and achievement in schools. In *Children's play and learning: Perspectives and policy implications,* eds. E. Klugman & S. Smilansky, 18–42. New York: Teachers College Press.

Souto-Manning, M. 2010. Family involvement: Challenges to consider, strengths to build on. *Young Children* 65 (2): 82–88.

Stacey, S. 2009. *Emergent curriculum in early childhood settings: From theory to practice.* St. Paul, MN: Redleaf.

Stephenson, A. 2009. Stepping back to listen to Jeff: Conversations with a 2-year-old. *Young Children* 64 (4): 90–95.

Tabors, P.O. 2008. *One child, two languages: A guide for early childhood educators of children learning English as a second language.* 2d ed. Baltimore, MD: Paul H. Brookes.

Tardos, A., ed. 2007. *Bringing up and providing care for infants and toddlers in an institution.* Budapest, Hungary: Pikler-LoczyTarsasag.

Tarr, P. 2001. *Early childhood classrooms: What art educators can learn from Reggio Emilia.* Reston, VA: National Art Education Association.

Thompson, R.A. 2009. Doing what *doesn't* come naturally: The development of self-regulation. *Zero to Three* 30 (2): 33–39.

Turner-Vorbeck, T., & M.M. Marsh, eds. 2008. *Other kinds of families: Embracing diversity in schools.* New York: Teachers College Press.

U.S. Department of Health and Human Services. 2003, September. *The Head Start leaders guide to positive child outcomes.* Washington, DC: Administration for Children and Families, Head Start Bureau.

Van der Zande, I. 2010. *1, 2, 3… the toddler years: A practical guide for parents and caregivers.* 3d ed. Santa Cruz, CA: Toddler Press.

Vygotsky, L.S. [1934] 1986. *Thought and language.* Cambridge, MA: MIT Press.

Wardle, F. 1999. In praise of developmentally appropriate practice. *Young Children* 54 (6): 4–11.

Weitzman, E., & J. Greenberg. 2002. *Learning language and loving it: A guide to promoting children's social and language development in early childhood settings.* Toronto: Hanen Centre.

Wittmer, D., & S. Petersen. 2009. *Infant and toddler development and responsive program planning: A relationship-based approach.* 2d ed. Boston, MA: Pearson.

Youngquist, J., & B. Martínez-Griego. 2009. Learning in English, learning in Spanish: A Head Start program changes its approach. *Young Children* 64 (4): 92–99.

Zero to Three. 2008. *Caring for infants and toddlers in groups: Developmentally appropriate practice.* 2d ed. Washington, DC: Zero to Three.

Zero to Three. 2009. *Zero to Three* 30 (1). [Entire issue focuses on play]

Zigler, E., D. Singer & S. Bishop-Josef. 2004. *Children's play: The roots of reading.* Washington, DC: Zero to Three.

Websites

National Resource Center for Health and Safety in Child Care. Database of states' licensing requirements: http://nrc.uchsc.edu/STATES/states.htm.

U.S. Dept. of Health and Human Services. *Early Head Start Research and Evaluation Project (EHSRE), 1996–Current.* Washington, DC: Administration for Children and Families, Office of Planning, Research and Evaluation, Head Start Bureau. www.acf.hhs.gov/programs/opre/ehs/ehs_resrch/index.html.

Online documents

Bright Horizons Family Solutions. 2003. *Ready to respond: Emergency preparedness plan for early care and education centers.* Online: www.brighthorizons.com/talktochildren/docs/emergency_plan.doc.

Cummins, J. 2001. Bilingual children's mother tongue: Why is it important for education? *Sprogforum* 7 (19): 15–20. Online: www.fiplv.org/Issues/CumminsENG.pdf.

Espinosa, L.M. 2008. *Challenging common myths about young English language learners.* New York: Foundation for Child Development. Online: www.fcd-us.org/sites/default/files/MythsOfTeachingELLsEspinosa.pdf.

IRA (International Reading Association) & NAEYC. 1998. *Learning to read and write: Developmentally appropriate practices for young children.* Joint Position Statement. Washington, DC: NAEYC. Online: www.naeyc.org/positionstatements. Also in Neuman, Copple & Bredekamp 2000.

NAEYC. 1995. Responding to linguistic and cultural diversity: Recommendations for effective early childhood education. Position Statement. Washington, DC: Author. Online: www.naeyc.org/positionstatements.

NAEYC. 2005, April. NAEYC code of ethical conduct. Position Statement. Washington, DC: Author. Online: www.naeyc.org/positionstatements.

NAEYC. 2009. Developmentally appropriate practice in early childhood programs serving children from birth through age 8. Position Statement. Washington, DC: Author. Online: www.naeyc.org/positionstatements.

Key Resources on Developmentally Appropriate Practice

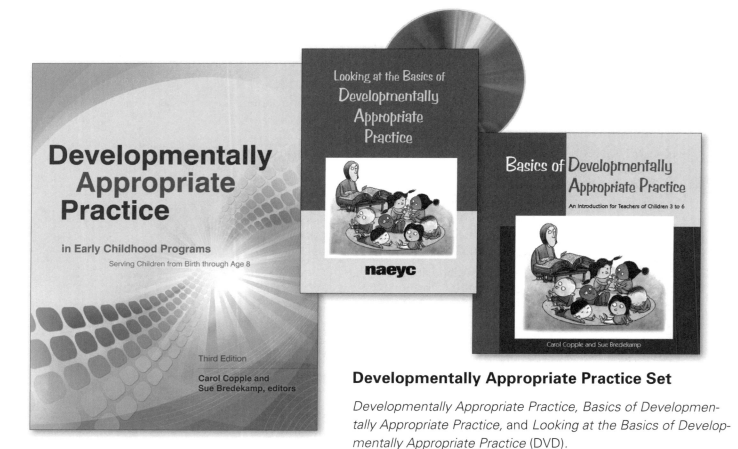

Developmentally Appropriate Practice Set

Developmentally Appropriate Practice, Basics of Developmentally Appropriate Practice, and *Looking at the Basics of Developmentally Appropriate Practice* (DVD).

Order #: 3752

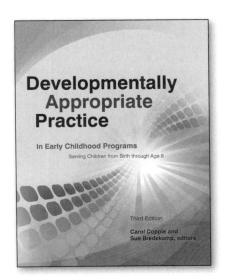

Developmentally Appropriate Practice in Early Childhood Programs Serving Children from Birth through Age 8 (3d ed.)

Carol Copple & Sue Bredekamp, eds.

Since the first edition in 1987, NAEYC's book *Developmentally Appropriate Practice in Early Childhood Programs* has been an essential resource for the early child care field. Now fully revised and expanded, the 2009 version comes with a supplementary CD containing readings on key topics, plus video examples showing developmentally appropriate practice in action. Based on what the research says about development, learning, and effective practices, as well as what experience tells us about teaching intentionally, *DAP* articulates the principles that should guide our decision making. Chapters describe children from birth through age 8 in detail, with extensive examples of appropriate practice for infant/toddler, preschool, kindergarten, and primary levels.

Order #: 375

Looking at the Basics of Developmentally Appropriate Practice (DVD)

A great fit with the *Basics* book (#259) and versatile enough to be shown as part of any beginner level discussion of DAP. Some instructors will want to show it when learners are using *Developmentally Appropriate Practice* (#375) or other texts. Children ages 3–6 are the focus. *Produced by NAEYC.* 41 min.

Order #: 861

TO PLACE AN ORDER:

Toll Free 1-800-424-2460

Order online
www.naeyc.org/store

Join NAEYC and Save on these and other Resources.